The Man Who Sold Nelson's Column

# The Man Who Sold Nelson's Column

## *And Other Scottish Frauds and Hoaxes*

DANE LOVE

**BIRLINN**

First published in 2007 by
Birlinn Limited
West Newington House
10 Newington Road
Edinburgh
EH9 1QS

*www.birlinn.co.uk*

ISBN13: 978 1 84158 612 0
ISBN10: 1 84158 612 9

British Library Cataloguing-in-Publication Data
A catalogue record for this book is available from the British Library

Typeset by Textype
Printed and bound by Antony Rowe Ltd, Chippenham

# Contents

# List of Illustrations

# Introduction

Sir Walter Scott, in his epic poem *Marmion*, wrote the classic lines, 'Oh what a tangled web we weave, when first we practise to deceive.' The warning is one that many of those in this book should perhaps have heeded, prior to carrying out their deceptions. Many of the people in this book perhaps began their adventures for a bit of a laugh, but as time passed, they found it ever more difficult to turn back.

There are hundreds of accounts of frauds and hoaxes that have taken place over the centuries in Scotland. Some of them have been obvious, perhaps pranks performed by students as part of Rag Week, others were jokes that were played on All Fools' Day, or 'Huntigowk' as it is (or was) known in Scotland. Others have been acted out by people who wished that they lived the lifestyle of their alter-ego, be it someone in a different career or social class.

An amusing tale appeared in one of my local newspapers about an unemployed fisherman who lived in a south Ayrshire village. He had a keen interest in the police, and decided that he would dress up as a policeman. The man, who was 21 at the time, acquired a uniform and hat. He cut out the thistle logo from Strathclyde Police's newspaper and stuck it to a card along with his own photograph, creating a fake identity card. With no work to go to, the bogus bobby went on patrol, looking for petty criminals. He is known to have entered a school playground, warning the children of the dangers of drugs. He maintained his deception for nine months, until he decided to move up a gear, and in December 2003 he drove his battered old car to a nearby town, where he put a toy siren on the roof. At the beach he warned children about their behaviour, but they were not fooled, and the real police were called. At Ayr Sheriff Court he later admitted three charges of impersonating a police officer.

In Edinburgh, on 19 August 2006, two young men dressed up as policemen and drove around in an Alfa Romeo car. They spotted a young woman driving at a speed that they decided was excessive. One of them attached a flashing blue light to the windscreen and followed her. The woman assumed it was an unmarked police car and pulled over. The man spoke to the driver and warned her about her speed before allowing her to continue. After a while the girl and her passengers realised that the policeman did not seem to be dressed properly, and they decided that there was something funny about the whole incident. They informed the police, who managed to track down the bogus policemen and arrest them. Apparently they had carried out the trick to impress a girl. They pled guilty at court in the spring of 2007.

An older hoax took place in Dalkeith on 26 September 1922. It was a time of high unemployment, and there were many men in the town looking for work. A man appeared in the town's High Street claiming he represented a firm working in Heriot, 12 miles away. He was looking to take on around 70 men to dig a track along which telephone cables were to be laid. Interest was rife, and he quickly gathered enough labourers. They were to be paid one shilling and one penny per hour, they would be provided with transport from Dalkeith to Heriot and back each week, and during the week they would have accommodation within huts at the site. Soon many others came looking for him, and it was reckoned that he actually employed between 80 and 100 men. On the Tuesday morning two buses arrived as promised and the men piled on board, many bringing their own picks and shovels. It was a happy bunch that made their way to Heriot, some not having had work for many years. However, at Heriot their spirit was quickly dowsed. The company that was digging the cable track had no knowledge of the extra workers. Dick Brothers, whose buses had been booked, discovered that they had no idea who would pay for them, and the police were called. The foreman at Heriot recognised the description of the hoaxer as being of a man who had given up his job with them on Monday.

These three tales seem fairly tame compared with some of the great financial frauds that have been perpetrated over the years. The largest fraud in Scotland's criminal history was engineered by Alison Anders, a senior accounts officer for Britoil at their Aberdeen headquarters. Anders discovered how lax the firm was with its financial arrangements and, with the aid of her boyfriend Royston Allen, a married company director, arranged for a payment of £23,331,996 to be transferred from Britoil's account into one that Anders had set up in Switzerland on 29 June 1988. Anders' attention to detail caught her out: she telexed specific instructions on how the funds should be transferred, but the teller at the Glasgow bank had never seen such an authorisation before. The teller asked her boss for advice and the transaction was referred to Britoil for clarification. In the meantime Shell and Esso, who were partners with Britoil in the lease of an oil rig, which the payment was for, queried the amount and the deal was suspended. Alison Anders panicked, knowing that the cash was now in her secret account. She made her way to Abu Dhabi using a false passport, where she met up with Royston Allen. BBC Television's *Crimewatch* aired an appeal to anyone who knew where Anders was, but nothing came of it. Alison escaped to America, but eventually the police tracked her down. She and Allen were tried for fraud in September 1989 and both were sentenced to five years, though this was reduced on appeal to four years. On their release they set up home together in the north of Scotland.

Living a life that is not yours appears to be a fairly common thing in Scotland, as will appear from the following pages. Perhaps the romance of being a Highland laird, or the aura of having a title, attracts a certain type of person. In this book there are various accounts of fraudsters who have adopted titles, from knighthoods to baronies, and convinced others that their title is genuine. Another is the story of the Australian, 'Lord' Battenberg, who took on the lease of Dunfallandy House, near Pitlochry, in 2005. Dunfallandy is the ancestral seat of the Fergusson family and Iain Stewart-Fergusson decided that it would make financial sense to lease their house to another tenant. They thought their luck was in when Andrew Battenberg agreed to pay them £5,000 per annum for the lease of the house, but he failed to come up with the cash, despite having lived there for some time. He even arranged for £35,000 worth of restoration work to be done, but only paid the builder around one-third of the total bill. Investigations later discovered that Battenberg was only a lord by purchase, having acquired the title 'Lord Andrew of Craigstown' from Lord Kilbracken for £5,000. His claims of kinship with various royal families were spurious, and there was even a rumour that he was a love-child of the Duke of Edinburgh. A trail of debt reaching across Britain and Australia forced Stewart-Fergusson to take Battenberg to court to have him evicted from Dunfallandy and the ten-year lease cancelled. Even Battenberg's chauffeur at Pitlochry sued him for £12,000 worth of outstanding debts.

Another hoax of some merit is the story of Anton Krashny, an artist who was fabricated during the 1974 Edinburgh Festival. Television broadcasters Clarke Tait and Joan Bakewell had been commissioned to present a programme on the festival, and once it was finished they held a party to celebrate. At the event was a junior researcher who had annoyed them much of the time the show was being produced – apparently he knew everything and everyone but did little actual work and invited himself to numerous productions which he boasted about afterwards. At the party Clarke Tait was so fed up of his pompous manner that he winked at Joan Bakewell and asked the researcher if he had seen the Krashny exhibition. The researcher fell for it hook, line and sinker, and claimed that he had, and that it had been wonderful. Word spread around the party, and soon the rest of the guests were discussing the exhibition and artist that didn't exist. As the years passed, it became a game to try to see how many times the guests who were 'in the know' could get Krashny's name in the papers, and they later formed a festival celebration of his life, the Krashny Dinner. In 1980 Krashny even appeared on the front page of the Glasgow *Evening Times* which reported 'Top Pole Flees to Safety', an account of how he was hoping to gain political asylum in Scotland. Author Roddy Martine stated that Krashny was created as 'a conspiracy to mock people who take the Festival too seriously.'

Hoaxers are of all ages, from youths to pensioners. The tale of a juvenile hoaxer dates back to 1925. A 13-year-old Glasgow schoolboy was found lying in an ash-pit in the vicinity of Jamieson Street in the city's Govanhill. The lad was found by a woman who was going to empty her ash-pan. The boy's hands and feet were tied together, string was wrapped around his neck, and his nostrils had been plugged. It had been raining, and the boy was soaking. At first the woman thought that he was a ragged child, asleep, with no home to go to, but she soon discovered that he was tied up. The finder quickly alerted the authorities and the boy, who was in an exhausted condition, was conveyed to the Victoria Infirmary. When he had been cleaned up, he said that he had been attacked by two men who robbed him of four shillings. They then bound him and left him lying in the ash-pit. The police found the story quite strange, and returned to interrogate him further. At length the lad, John Miller, admitted that the whole thing had been a hoax. He had read a detective novel entitled *The Australian Wild* and decided that it would be great to create a sensation about himself.

Forging banknotes and coins has been taking place in Scotland ever since notes and coins were introduced. Within this book are three accounts of forgers from different periods, but there are hundreds more. One of some significance was Thomas Watling (1762–*c*.1814), who was born in Dumfries. Watling's parents died when he was young and he was brought up by his maiden aunt. He set up his own academy, teaching 'drawing to ladies and gentlemen for a guinea a month'. He was arrested on 27 December 1788 and tried for forging at least 12 Bank of Scotland one-guinea notes. He claimed that they were only created as an experiment and that they were done in vermilion and not black ink, so could not be circulated. Prior to the trial on 14 April 1789 he petitioned for transportation, knowing that he was likely to be executed. This was agreed and he was sentenced to 14 years in Botany Bay, Australia. For a time he was held in a prison ship in Plymouth harbour before being sent abroad on the good ship *Pitt* in June 1791. He temporarily escaped in South Africa when the ship docked to take on more supplies, but was captured within 15 days and held in an African prison for seven months. He was then taken to Port Jackson in Australia, arriving on 7 October 1792. Whilst there he became the first professional artist in the convict colony and his paintings sold to wealthy collectors. He wrote numerous letters to his aunt in Dumfries, which were published around 1794. He was given a conditional pardon in 1796, becoming absolute the following year. He eventually could afford to return to Scotland, travelling by way of Calcutta (1801–3). In Edinburgh on 10 January 1806 he was charged again with forgery, it being claimed that he had forged at least seven £5 Bank of Scotland notes, but amazingly, considering the evidence against him, he was released as the case was 'not proven'. He then moved to London, but probably died shortly thereafter from cancer. The

British Museum has a large collection of Watling paintings and drawings, and he is a celebrated artist in Australia.

Mention was made of students' hoaxes. One of the most successful was the story of 'Miss F.N. Tynne' and 'Mr L.S. Dee', which took place in September 1933. This started as a small-scale hoax in aid of charity, but in the end it deceived thousands of people. The students placed a note in a Port Glasgow paper announcing that Miss Tynne and her mechanic, Mr Dee, had flown from Vancouver across the Atlantic on a record-breaking attempt, taking four days, but that she had crashed on the moors above Port Glasgow. The notice in the paper announced that Miss Tynne would make a public announcement about the flight at Greenock Central Station on Thursday 28 September. Despite their strange names, the public became excited at the story. Some people called at the hospital with gifts, the police were inundated with requests for information, and souvenir hunters walked the Port Glasgow moors in search of the wreck. Captain John Houston of the Scottish Flying Club was kept busy answering queries, and some newspapers were fooled into writing about the 'air disaster' at Port Glasgow. The students had been successful in their hoax and thousands turned up at the station, where they were asked for donations for the hospital charity that the students were collecting for. On the night, two students, dressed as the 'fliers', were feted in the town, mainly for pulling off one of the great hoaxes of the day. A student spokesman stated that, 'It has been a great stunt; in fact it has been the stunt of stunts so far as students' charity days are concerned.'

In writing this book I have had assistance from a variety of people, all of whom are due an acknowledgment, and I extend my thanks to Hugh Edgar, Brian Innes, Hope Marston, Moira Rothnie and Douglas Skelton, as well as the staff of the many libraries that dutifully answered my queries and searched out material on my behalf.

There are numerous tales of hoaxes and frauds from Scotland and I hope that the reader enjoys the following selection.

Dane Love
Auchinleck, 2007

# 1

## The Monumental Salesman: Arthur Furguson

It was a bright sunny morning in 1923 and a rather dapper-looking man, Arthur Furguson, was making his way through London's Trafalgar Square. He spotted a tourist standing gazing in awe at the tall pillar of Nelson's Column, which had been erected between 1840–3 in commemoration of the great admiral, Horatio Nelson (1758–1805), victor of the Battle of Trafalgar. Standing 169 feet in height, the column comprises a fluted granite pillar rising from a base protected by large stone lions, sculpted by Sir Edwin Landseer. On the uppermost point of the pillar is a larger-than-life, 17-foot-tall statue of Nelson.

Whatever possessed Furguson to decide to play a joke on the unsuspecting tourist is not known, but he was quick-witted enough to announce to him that he was the official guide to the square, and began to weave a strange story which the tourist swallowed, hook, line and sinker. The tourist, a rich American from Iowa who was on holiday in the city, listened reverently as Furguson spoke.

At first Furguson told how Admiral Nelson was one of the great British heroes of his time, who lost his sight in one eye during battle, and was mortally wounded at Trafalgar, the decisive battle of the Napoleonic Wars.

Furguson's mind began to elaborate the story quite wildly as he realised the Iowan was lapping up every word. He explained that Britain was still in a dire financial condition since the First World War, and that the Great Depression was taking an economic toll on the government of the day. Unfortunately the country was suffering from considerable debt, and it had been decided to sell off some of the more valuable memorials and museum pieces that would help raise funds quickly. Nelson's Column was one such heirloom that was currently up for sale.

The American remained interested, indeed very interested. He was desirous of acquiring the monument and shipping it back home to Iowa, where it would become a great symbol of his wealth. He asked Furguson the price of the column.

'The government is looking for £6,000,' Furguson told him. He continued to explain that he, the official guide to the square, had also been given the task of finding a suitable purchaser from the many inquiries that had been made. 'The prospective purchaser would have to keep the whole sale in total secrecy,' he continued, 'and no announcement was to be made by either side until the deal had been completed. The government is also insistent that the column should not be sold to just anyone, and that the purchaser should guarantee its future dignity.'

The Iowan told Furguson that he was keen to purchase the memorial, and that he felt he had all the credentials required by the government. He would have the memorial dismantled and shipped to America, where it would be re-erected exactly as it was in London. Furguson asked him where the column would go, how it would be moved and rebuilt, and what access the public would have to it, for it was still a much-loved landmark in London. The American answered the questions, and asked if there was a chance that he could be considered as a purchaser. He eventually begged Furguson to sell the monument to him.

Arthur Furguson told the American that he felt he could be the right person to purchase the landmark, and that the answers to his questions had convinced him that he was worthy of consideration. However, there was already a long list of prospective purchasers whose names he had passed to the Ministry of Works. Nevertheless, he told him that he would consult his superiors and return with an answer as soon as possible. He left the American standing in the square, looking at the memorial, wondering if it could be his fairly soon.

Within minutes Furguson returned bearing good news. He was delighted to tell the American that the government agency would be happy to accept his offer and that they were very keen to have the sale completed as soon as possible. The Iowan produced a chequebook from his jacket and wrote one payable to Furguson. In return, Furguson was able to supply him with a receipt. Furguson continued the conversation for some time, and was able to supply the American with the name of a suitable firm of monumental masons who could carry out the dismantling and shipping of the memorial for him. After some time, the two men shook hands on the deal and parted.

It was only when the American contacted the contractors to arrange for the dismantling of Nelson's Column that he discovered that something was amiss. The builders listened incredulously as he asked them to quote for the dismantling of the column and shipping to North America. They inquired why he wanted to know, assuming it was a purely hypothetical inquiry, perhaps trying to answer some sort of query posed in a newspaper or quiz. When the American insisted that he had just bought the memorial they told him that they didn't think that was possible, for they had no knowledge of the column being put on the market, and did not think that it ever would be. They told him that he must have been the victim of a fraud.

The American was still convinced that he was right, however, and contacted Scotland Yard. The policemen advised him that the contractors were right, that the monument had never been on sale, and that he had indeed been hoodwinked. They took as many details as they could from him about Furguson, and began an inquiry. Furguson, by this time, had disappeared with his cheque.

Arthur Furguson was born in Glasgow. He became an actor, which he was later to find useful in his dealings with unsuspecting victims. He was not particularly successful on the stage, and at the time he was selling Nelson's Column he was only acting minor roles with a touring company of players. He had previously toured Scotland and the north of England with repertory companies, playing in melodramatic productions. In one of these plays he acted the part of an American who had been cheated by a conman. Perhaps this part was instrumental in him turning to conning others.

Arthur Furguson was amazed at just how gullible certain members of the public were, and he repeated his con a number of times. He met another American and was able to persuade him to pay him £1,000 to buy Big Ben, the clock tower attached to the Houses of Parliament.

Another sale that he pulled off was the royal family's residence of Buckingham Palace, accepting a down payment of £2,000 from an American tycoon. However, when the new 'owner' arrived at the gates of the palace and was refused entry, he realised that he had been double-crossed.

Furguson is also thought to have travelled to Paris, where he was able to con a visiting American into buying the Eiffel Tower for its scrap-metal value. He had explained the tower was only a temporary structure erected for the International Exhibition of Paris in 1889, and that it was now becoming unsafe and needed to be dismantled.

These cons were only the ones that came to light, where the victims contacted the police to report Furguson. No doubt there were many other cases of fraud where the victim, on finding out that he had been 'done' was too embarrassed to take his case to the authorities, for fear of looking stupid.

Within 18 months or so of the Nelson's Column sale, Arthur Furguson decided that the trail was getting too hot for his liking.

He was determined to move on and decided that America was the place for him. Accordingly, he moved across the Atlantic in 1925.

Probably Furguson's first major con in America was to offer the lease of the White House to a Texan cattle rancher. Furguson had met him and explained that the American government wished to increase funds without raising taxes. Wishing to hold on to their assets, the White House would still be owned by the United States, but it was being offered to let on a 99-year lease at $100,000 per annum. The wealthy Texan jumped at the chance of being the sole occupant of the national monument and paid the first year's rent in advance to Furguson. He was never to see him again, and of course the White House was never leased to anyone.

On another occasion Furguson met a very rich Australian from Sydney who was in New York on business. They were in the vicinity of the city's harbour, and Furguson began to explain that there were plans to develop New York harbour, but that the Statue of Liberty was in the way of the new wider entrance for the super-ships that the city was expecting to attract. The statue as it stood may have had considerable sentimental value to the residents of the 'Big Apple', but the US State Department were keen that the harbour developments would not be compromised, and were proposing a newer, larger monument as part of their scheme. Accordingly the statue was being offered for sale to the first person to offer $100,000 deposit and the means of transporting it away.

The Australian was very keen to acquire such an icon, and struck a deal with Furguson. He proposed transporting the statue to Sydney, where it would be erected at the entrance to the harbour there, much in the same way that it stood at the mouth of Manhattan harbour. Furguson spent some time with the Australian, taking him on a tour of the tower. However, the Australian had some difficulty in raising the money needed for the quick sale that Furguson demanded. He tried various sources for the cash, but it was taking him a few days to tie the money down.

Over this period Furguson hung around the Australian to ensure that he did not mention the sale to anyone. As time passed, Furguson became impatient to get the deal done and his impatience became apparent to the Australian, who began to think the whole deal looked suspicious.

The Australian businessman went to the New York police to report the case. He had with him his camera, in which was a photograph of both him and Furguson, taken by a passer-by, with the Statue of Liberty in the background. The film was processed, and the police now had a detailed picture of what the conman looked like. They had been looking for Furguson for some time, and this was the vital evidence that they required. The Australian was also able to lead them to Furguson, and he was immediately arrested.

Furguson was tried for fraudulent activity and found guilty. The judge sentenced him to five years in the city penitentiary.
Furguson served his five years in gaol, being released in 1930. He left New York and headed west, settling in Los Angeles. He was able to purchase a luxurious house in one of the better parts of the city with funds he had stored away prior to his prison term.

Furguson continued to con the public, on a smaller scale, but was never caught for it again. From his swindles he was able to live a comfortable lifestyle, before he died in 1938.

And so ended the life of one of the great fraudsters of all time. His story appears in a variety of books, on websites from around the world, and his name is regularly mentioned in newspapers, when stories of con artists are written. But facts about Furguson have proved illusive. He, in fact, is the hoax, for he never existed, and his massive frauds never took place, and the fraud has been played out on those who have written about him ever since.

There is no contemporary record of Furguson's frauds, and the newspapers of the period make no reference to any of his major deceits. Even when he was caught by the police and imprisoned, what would have been a major story in both America and Britain was not reported in the press. There are also no reports of Furguson's supposed frauds at the time they took place, despite their ambitious scale.

In America, research into Furguson turned up nothing, other than recent versions of the story related here. In France, the man who sold the Eiffel Tower was in fact 'Count' Victor Lustig (1890–1947), who is famous for a number of con tricks. Perhaps Furguson's initials indicate that his story is nothing but an elaborate April Fool, one that has been 'lifted' by hacks and writers and replayed throughout the world.

# 2

# *The Bogus Laird:*
# *Anthony Williams*

The village of Tomintoul appears to be nothing remarkable. Located 13 miles south-east of Grantown-on-Spey, in the Banffshire Highlands, it was established as a planned settlement in 1775 by the 4th Duke of Gordon to re-house crofters removed from the land. The long main street, almost one mile in length, is lined with single-storey houses, fronting directly onto the street. These houses were originally occupied by weavers, the new trade that the laird wished his tenants to take up. A grid pattern of streets was planned, with the intention of creating a thriving town, but other than a few lanes off the main street, Tomintoul never grew beyond a village. Its name is better known today for being at one end of the infamous Cock Bridge to Tomintoul road, which ascends to almost 2,100 feet above sea level at the Lecht, and consequently is usually the first main road in Britain to become blocked by winter snows.

Tomintoul in the 1980s was suffering from high unemployment, with cutbacks in forestry and farming affecting the village. Tourists were sparse, the Lecht ski areas suffering from a lack of snow, or in many cases, too much snow, so much that skiers couldn't get there! The population was diminishing to around

500 and as was the case in many Highland communities, young people were moving elsewhere to find work and set up home. The village seemed to be forgotten, missing out on any tourism that existed in the Highlands, and becoming abandoned by its own residents.

Then, in 1987, things began to take a turn for the better. An English couple, Anthony and Kay Williams, purchased a semi-derelict house, Mallory Cottage, for £7,000, and set about renovating it. They used local tradesmen, and when the renovation was complete they had spent almost £400,000. The work was greatly appreciated by local builders, and they were delighted to find that Anthony Williams planned further employment for them.

Anthony Williams presented himself as Lord Williams, for he was the owner of a Scottish feudal barony. These titles are relics of the time when the early kings granted baronies to local lairds so that they would police the area and ensure support for the Crown. The titles are not hereditary, and can be sold from person to person. Although they are recognised by the Lord Lyon King of Arms, Scotland's supreme judge on heraldic matters, they do not entitle the bearer to sit in the House of Lords. Anthony Williams' title, Baron of Chirnside, a large village in Berwickshire, was purchased by him at an auction of baronies and English Lords of the Manor, held in London.

On completing the renovation of Mallory Cottage, Lord Williams commenced a buying spree. He acquired vacant properties in the village and spent considerable amounts of money doing them up. Local tradesmen became his followers, for they were delighted to be receiving as much work as they could cope with. Many of the properties were run down, and some had been in danger of being demolished.

One of the buildings Lord Williams bought was the former Campbell's Corner Shop, distinguished by a circular clock face on a corner turret. This general store had closed down but later functioned as a restaurant. Williams purchased the building and commenced restoration work. It reopened in 1989 as the Clockhouse Restaurant, a French-style bistro, serving good food, with an in-house bakery. In total, £500,000 had been spent on its conversion.

Major restoration was carried out by Williams on the Gordon Arms Hotel, the traditional hotel that stands in The Square, at the centre of the village. The hotel was placed on the market, and Williams is known to have paid well in excess of its value. Despite this, he spent a further £2 million installing new facilities, furniture and decoration. A massive granite building, it is three storeys in height, with a fourth floor incorporated in the attic. When it reopened, it was again one of the Highlands' most stylish hotels, complete with luxurious accommodation and quality service.

Anthony Williams wanted one of the best managers he could get for his hotel. Williams was a timeshare owner at the Hilton Craigendarroch complex, located on the edge of Ballater, on Royal Deeside. There he cultivated the friendship of David Abdy, restaurant manager, whom he persuaded to move to the Gordon Arms Hotel and take over the running of the hotel and restaurant. Mr Abdy was able to turn the fortunes of the hotel around, and he was even made a director of Williams' holding company.

Not only did David Abdy move to Tomintoul, his parents, John and Barbara Abdy, decided to join him. They purchased a bungalow and took over the village post office and general store on the west side of The Square.

Attached to the Gordon Hotel, as it was renamed, was the public bar, known as the Grouse's Nest. Williams totally renovated this, gutting the site and installing new fixtures and fittings. The bar was filled with a fine selection of malt and blended whiskies, Tomintoul being located just over the hill from Glen Livet, one of the country's most famous whisky-producing areas.

Other buildings purchased by Williams included the former bus station in Conglass Lane, the old fire station and a few other cottages. Another building he acquired was the Old Manse of Creggan, a rather fine three-storey house, formerly the home of the local minister. This building was used as the headquarters of his local empire, and it was Williams' intention to retire to this house.

Lord Williams' purchases also included a holiday villa in Spain, bought at a cost of £200,000, where he often spent time relaxing in the sun.

The new business that Anthony, or Tony as he was known to his friends, Williams brought to Tomintoul was welcomed by the locals. He created employment for builders, plumbers, electricians, decorators and a whole host of other tradesmen, who had been finding times hard in the upland village. His restoration of the hotel and bar and creation of a new restaurant brought much-needed trade and tourists to the community, and as they stopped to use the facilities, they also spent money in other villagers' businesses.

Williams grouped his businesses under an umbrella organisation known as Tomintoul Enterprises Ltd.

Even by throwing money at the businesses, Anthony Williams could not make them pay. Those who were close to the businesses could see that they were not bringing in a sufficient income to keep them going. However, Lord Williams seemed to have deep pockets, and supplying money did not appear to be a problem.

The locals knew that Williams worked in London, that he was something of a 'big-noise', but that what he did was top secret. Some knew that he was connected with Scotland Yard, and others were privy to his claim that he had inherited a small fortune from a distant relative in Scandinavia.

Anthony Williams *did* in fact work for Scotland Yard, but his salary was not in the top league of earners. He was paid around £32,000 per annum as a deputy establishment officer. He did know some secrets, but they were no big deal. What he did have access to, importantly, was a police charity fund. Williams had a few debts to clear up, and he found it easy to access the funds.

With his debtors cleared, and no one in the police force aware of what he had done, Williams found it very tempting to access further accounts.

At Scotland Yard, Williams had been given the job of supervising a secret cash account that was to be used to fund a special operation to fight organised crime. The money was supposed to be used to pay for tip-offs and bungs, and so secret was the fund that only Williams knew where the cash was spent. This was to be his undoing, for it became simple to send funds to his own accounts. Indeed, so easy did it become that he is known to have spent over £5 million of police money over a period of 11 years. Only £2.5 million of the fund was used in the fight against crime.

Anthony Williams had separated from his first wife, and had found a new love, Kay, whom he was to marry. She was unaware of his secret fund and like the locals in Tomintoul was under the impression that he had inherited his wealth. Williams appeared to be a cheery fellow. He wore glasses and when he was dressed up for a night out he often wore a kilt with a green jacket.

Williams' siphoning of cash from the police account went unnoticed by Scotland Yard and the Metropolitan Police. How long this would have been the case cannot be guessed. It was the local branch of the Clydesdale Bank in Tomintoul that brought about his downfall. Williams was passing a variety of strange cheques through his accounts there, and the manager became suspicious of the source of Williams' vast fortune. The manager contacted Scotland Yard's fraud department, and a secret investigation was undertaken. The extent of the massive scam was soon apparent.

Whilst Williams was down in England, living at his New Malden, Surrey, home, police officers knocked at his door and arrested him. He was charged with fraud and embezzlement and taken to the local police station.

Anthony Williams was taken to the Old Bailey courthouse in London in May 1995. At the end of the trial the judge summed up by recounting how Williams stole money and it was 'for personal advantage in a luxurious lifestyle and the acquisition of properties and business. The aggrandisement was shown in the assumption of a baronial title.'

He pled guilty to the 19 charges that had been put before him, and in addition he asked for a further 535 cases of fraud or embezzlement to be taken into consideration.

Williams was sentenced to seven and a half years in gaol. He sat quietly as the sentence was read out. By his side were a few belongings in a bag, as though he was sure that he would be spending some time in prison. However, when the length of his sentence was read out, Williams was stunned.

The locals of Tomintoul suffered with the loss of their local benefactor. When his businesses were closed down a number of local tradesmen and suppliers were left with outstanding accounts of around £200,000.

At the Gordon Hotel, manager David Abdy managed to do a deal with the National Westminster Bank and was able to keep the business operating. He continued to run the hotel for a few years, but it was eventually put on the market and was acquired by McKever Hotels.

The Metropolitan Police were also placed under considerable scrutiny following Williams' sentence. It was questioned why so much money was placed in the trust of one individual, and why it was so easy for him to siphon off such significant funds from under the noses of the top police officers in the country. A press release issued by the commissioner stated:

Confidentiality must never be an excuse for inadequate financial controls. Immediately the fraud came to light, a full audit was launched of all financial procedures and controls in respect of confidential operations. The review had established that there was no evidence of any other theft, corruption or fraud and there were no similar weaknesses in the financial controls of other accounts.

When Williams' property was sold off only around £1 million of the £5 million he had stolen was recuperated. The rest had been spent on extravagant restoration work on buildings that were unlikely to fetch what had been spent on them. Even Williams' baronial title was taken from him and sold to the current Baroness of Chirnside, Ethel Patricia Hewitt Kirby.

The story of Lord Williams was one that caught the attention of a Hollywood filmmaker. Phoenix Pictures, which had previously produced *The Thin Red Line*, had proposed telling the tale in a comedic light in a film to be entitled *The Laird*. Mel Smith was to be the director and shooting was planned for the summer of 1999. However, the film was cancelled before a single shot was taken.

# 3

# The Monster Hoaxes:
# The Loch Ness Monster

Everyone knows that the Loch Ness monster is a real beast of some sort, one that lives in the deep, deep waters of Loch Ness. St Columba was probably the earliest known person to have seen the monster, which appeared before him in the year AD 565. A man had been swimming across the River Ness when the monster rose out of the water and bit him, causing him to die. Columba, according to his early biographer, Abbot Adamnan, arrived at the time of the burial. Columba sent a swimmer to fetch the man's boat, but the monster appeared once more, whereupon Columba held up his hands and shouted, 'Think not to go further nor touch thou that man. Quick! Go Back!' The monster ignored the terrified man in the water and turned around, much to the relief of the crowd who were watching, and who were converted to Christianity.

In 1933 the A82 road was built along the west side of the loch, after which sightings of the monster increased considerably. Since that time there have been hundreds of glimpses of the monster, in many cases just parts of its body mysteriously appearing above the surface of the loch, spotted for a few minutes before disappearing once more into the murky depths. However, there have been a number of so-called sightings and photographs taken of 'Nessie', as the monster is affectionately known, that have turned out to be hoaxes, often only being confirmed as such many years after the image was first released.

One of the greatest hoaxes associated with the Loch Ness monster is the photograph that was taken on 1 April 1934, and which has subsequently become known as the 'Surgeon's Photograph'. The date was not taken as being indicative of the dubiety of the picture at the time, for the photograph was presented to the world as genuine. According to the story Lieutenant Colonel Robert Kenneth Wilson and a friend, Maurice Chambers, were on the shores of Loch Ness when they spotted the monster's head rearing out of the waters of the loch. Wilson was able to take two photographs before the monster disappeared back below the surface of the water. One of these was to play a significant part in promoting the story of the monster, and was used for the following 60 years.

The photograph was published, and caused a sensation throughout the world. It showed a small head and slender neck projecting through the water's surface. In appearance, the head of the monster matched contemporary thinking on what the monster looked like – something along the lines of a plesiosaur, a name that means 'near reptile.' It was claimed that this was 'the most conclusive evidence yet that a prehistoric monster lives in Loch Ness.'

At the time the photographs were taken Robert Wilson worked as a gynaecologist, having a practice located near Harley Street in London. He had various degrees to his name and was a fellow of the Royal College of Surgeons, all of which lent credence to his honesty. Indeed, Wilson claimed that he had never heard of the Loch Ness monster prior to his visit to the loch, when he was able to capture it on film.

The photograph was supposed to have been taken at a spot around two miles north of Invermoriston, near to Alltsigh, on the western shores of the loch. Wilson and Chambers spotted the monster out in the loch, about 250 yards from the shore. Wilson grabbed his camera and fired off four shots, two of which failed to capture anything. Two frames, however, showed the monster's head and neck, and one of these pictures became an iconic representation of Nessie. The two images that caught the monster were similar, the second depicting the neck lower in the water, as though the monster was sinking deeper into the loch.

Wilson sent off his pictures to the *Daily Mail*, which published what became known as the 'surgeon's photograph' on 21 May 1934. The image was quickly replicated in newspapers and news bulletins around the world.

Involved in giving further weight to the photograph was Marmaduke A. Wetherell, who was noted at the time for being a big-game hunter. During the winter of 1933–4 he led a *Daily Mail*-sponsored expedition to Loch Ness, at which time he claimed that he would, once and for all, prove that the monster existed. He was quick to turn up evidence, but unfortunately, much of this turned out to be false.

One of the hoaxes Wetherell became involved with was the 'discovery' of large footprints on the side of the loch near to Fort Augustus. He made plaster casts of these and sent them off to the Natural History Museum in London to find out what had made them. A few sightings of the monster had taken place on the edge of the loch, indicating that it sometimes left the waters and ventured onto the land. The scientists at the museum analysed the casts and a fortnight after they were discovered announced to an eager audience what had made them – an umbrella stand that had been formed from the foot of a hippopotamus. Someone had been there before Wetherell and pulled the wool over his eyes.

Not everyone was convinced by Wilson's photograph. Alastair Boyd, who claimed to have seen the monster in 1979, and David Martin, a fellow monster hunter, were quick to dismiss the picture. They set about making a copy, fabricating a model of the monster and taking their own photograph to show just how easily it could be created. A dummy head and neck were affixed to a toy submarine, and this was put out into the loch. The resulting photographs appeared very similar to Wilson's picture of 1934.

Wilson and Chambers kept the secret of their hoax photograph for years. Wilson eventually confessed to a friend that the photographs were indeed a hoax, and that he had only intended them to be a practical joke. He shunned publicity for most of his life, so it was thought that he did not want to be interviewed and questioned every time the Loch Ness monster was spotted. But Wilson kept a low profile because he feared being found out, and he did not want to lose his professional reputation. He emigrated to Australia with his family, where he died in 1969. Wilson's youngest son later confirmed that the photograph had been a hoax. Marmaduke Wetherell's stepson, Christian Spurling, had also been involved in Wilson's con and confessed his part in the fabrication of the photograph to a close friend just before he died in March 1994. He claimed that he had set up the photograph using a toy submarine to tow a monster's head.

In 1993 the Discovery Channel produced a television programme that looked into the authenticity of Wilson's photograph, even though there had been a number of confessions of guilt by then. The programme assembled a number of photographic experts who studied the pictures and pronounced judgement on them. It was claimed that there was a white spot on the surface of the water just in front of the monster's neck, and that there were ripples coming from it, indicating that the neck was being pulled along.

In 1933 Bertram Mills, the celebrated circus owner, used a Loch Ness theme to promote his circus. He also caused something of a monster-hunting sensation when he offered £20,000 to anyone who could capture the monster. This was a massive reward, probably worth in the region of £3 million in 2007, and resulted in numerous visitors to the loch. Some went to fool others, and in 1934 a crocodile claw that had been placed by a prankster was discovered near Urquhart Castle.

Another photographer who hoaxed a number of pictures of the monster was Frank E. Searle. He was born in Staines, Middlesex, on 18 March 1921 and served as a sniper in the army for 18 years. He was injured in Palestine, losing the lower part of his left leg. On his demob he became a greengrocer in London. However, after reading *More than a Legend* by Constance Whyte, he became obsessed with the Loch Ness monster and decided to move to the side of the loch in June 1969. At first he stayed in a tent at Balachladoich farm, which is near to Dores, at the north-eastern end of the loch, remaining there for three years. He later moved into a field below Boleskine House, which was infamous for being the home of Aleister Crowley, a famous occultist, who claimed to have raised the devil in 1912, and who wrote a number of books on satanic practices.

Searle later acquired a blue-and-white caravan, which he had pitched at Lower Foyers. This caravan was given the rather grand-sounding title of 'Frank Searle Loch Ness Investigation Centre.' Visitors were entertained by Searle's account of monster-hunting expeditions, but the exhibition was mainly an egocentric one, for there was little more to see than a number of cuttings from newspapers that featured Searle himself, or else photographs of different parts of the loch, some with dubious sightings of the monster within them. Nevertheless, at one time he could claim that 20,000 visitors called at his 'information centre' in one year, and he received 2,000 letters from wellwishers. He did not charge for visits, but donations left helped him to survive.

Searle spent many hours searching for the monster, around 38,000 by his own calculation, and apparently caught sight of it on a number of occasions. His first photograph was taken on 27 July 1972, near to Balachladoich farm. This appeared in the 1 September edition of the *Daily Mail,* bringing him international acclaim. He was regularly interviewed on television, and he revelled in his new-found celebrity. However, he went on to produce a number of photographs over the period he spent at

Loch Ness, most of which have turned out to be fakes. It is thought that this was not Searle's original intention, and that he had arrived at the loch hoping to make his name by capturing a genuine image of the monster with his Box Brownie camera. However, failing to obtain a picture quickly enough, Searle resorted to producing fake ones.

Searle claimed that he had spotted the monster many times and had taken over 20 different pictures of it. Interest in the monster grew, and many people visited Searle's information centre, from where he subsequently published a quarterly newsletter, relating sightings and questioning many of the more scientific investigations into the existence of the monster.

In 1974 Nicholas Witchell, a television presenter, published a book entitled *The Loch Ness Story* in which he denounced Searle as a fake. In the book he details Searle's various pictures of the monster, and concludes that 'it is a regrettable fact which can be easily proved that these photographs have been tampered with.'

In 1976 Frank Searle had his own book published by Coronet, entitled, *Nessie, Seven Years in Search of the Monster*. This gave a history of sightings of Nessie, and included details of Searle's own life on the shores of the loch.

In February 1977 Searle was joined at his caravan by a Belgian woman, Lieve Peten, who claimed to be his assistant. Known as an 'Assistant Monster Huntress', Lieve helped Searle produce his newsletter. This was issued from April 1977 until December 1983. Lieve, however, left Loch Ness in 1979.

In the meantime, researchers began to question Searle's large collection of photographs, and soon he was exposed as a hoaxer. Any contact he had with the press from this point onwards was taken with a considerable pinch of salt, and he became ever more desperate to court publicity. One of his pictures of Nessie even included a UFO in the distant sky – a chance even more unlikely than taking a decent picture of the monster itself.

Searle was interviewed by Malcolm Robinson of Strange

Phenomena Investigations Scotland for the journal *Enigmas*. In it he claimed that he had seen Nessie 38 times, and that on one occasion 11 different people at three different locations saw the monster.

Searle wrote a second book on the Loch Ness monster which was to remain unpublished. Another researcher at Loch Ness, Adrian Shine, read the manuscript and claimed that some of the passages in it were defamatory, and also that much of the text was copied from other books that had already been published. Searle's publisher was notified of the concerns, and decided to cancel the contract. Searle was livid, and is reported as having said that he would be a 'thorn in the flesh' of Shine from that day onward. He failed to keep his word, however, for Searle disappeared and was not seen at the loch-side again.

Frank Searle left Loch Ness around 1983, disappearing from the limelight. It is thought that he became disillusioned with the lack of interest in his photographs, and was annoyed that other monster hunters were getting more publicity than he was. However, his story was used as the basis of a film entitled *Loch Ness*, starring Ted Danson, in which actor Keith Allen played Searle. Produced in Hollywood, the film was released in 1995.

In 2005 there were plans to make a documentary on the life of Frank Searle, and television producer Andrew Tullis tried to track him down. Searle's whereabouts were unknown and rumours circulated that he had either killed himself and was lying at the bottom of Loch Ness, or was spending time touring North America lecturing on monsters. Another theory claimed that he was searching for hidden treasure on ships wrecked in Cornwall. Others thought that he had found an interest in standing stones and other ancient ritual sites, and was off in search of them.

However, Searle had merely returned south to England, where he set up home, with a few cats, in a small flat in Fleetwood, Lancashire, in 1986. He kept a low profile from then on, and did not court any more publicity concerning the monster. In 1998 he suffered a stroke, which left much of his right-hand side paralysed. He spent some time in a wheelchair, but refused to go into a nursing home. Producer Tullis tracked down Searle but it was too late, for he died on 26 March 2005, aged 84. Nevertheless, Tullis made his film on Searle's life, entitled *The Man who Captured Nessie*, broadcast by Channel 4 in 2005.

What Searle did for the Loch Ness monster story has been looked at in several ways. Some say that his hoaxes did considerable harm to the science of cryptozoology, setting back sensible research. Others, however, were less critical, claiming that Searle's photographs raised the interest of the Loch Ness phenomena around the world and resulted in hundreds of serious researches by a variety of organisations. Some people just gave thanks for the boost to the local tourist industry that his publicity seeking provided.

In 2003 the Loch Ness monster made the headlines once more. A man had discovered the remains of four fossilized vertebrae on the shores of the loch and these were reported to the National Museum of Scotland. Gerald McSorley, a retired dealer in scrap metals from Stirling, had been at the loch and was walking along the shore. He tripped up at one point and landed in the water. As he climbed back out he discovered the four vertebrae, which still had some indication of their blood vessels and spinal column. McSorley recognized that the vertebrae were unusual, and sent them to the museum in Edinburgh.

Scientists at the museum quickly identified the fossils as being from a plesiosaur, a type of dinosaur that is thought to have roamed the earth around 100–200 million years ago. It is the type of dinosaur that Nessie has most often been associated with, having a long serpentine neck. Measuring around 35 feet from the tip of its head to the end of its tail, the plesiosaur was a fish-eating mammal that kept to the shallow waters along the coast. Nessie supporters claim that at some point a number of these creatures were trapped in Loch Ness when the sea receded. However, they are thought to have died out around 65 million years ago and Loch Ness did not become an enclosed lake until around ten thousand years ago, with the retreat of the last Ice Age.

Although scientists in Edinburgh confirmed that the fossilized vertebrae were indeed from a plesiosaur, they soon had their doubts. The vertebrae were encased in limestone rock but the natural rocks around Loch Ness are igneous or metamorphic. Inspection by microscope also revealed that the fossil had been drilled into by tiny marine organisms, the type that only exist in salt water. This information indicated that the fossil had originally been located on a seashore, and that someone had planted it at Loch Ness. Indeed, it was found near a lay-by, one of only a few places where the public road runs close to the loch.

# 4

# A Lost Half Million:
# The Burns Temple Hoax

On Wednesday 10 February 1904, the usual monthly meeting of
Kilmarnock Town Council was held in the council chambers in
the Town House, King Street. Provost James Hood stood up and
addressed the councillors sitting around the table and invited Mr
Middlemas, the town clerk, to read the correspondence. In his
hands was a single letter, which had been written by Mr Hew
Morrison of the Edinburgh Free Library. He was writing on
behalf of Mr Andrew Carnegie, the great philanthropist and
richest man in the world. The letter read:

> The Provost of Kilmarnock
> Dear Sir,
> I have just received word by this mail that Mr Carnegie, who was
> so deeply impressed with the progressive tendencies of
> Kilmarnock during his recent visit, has had under consideration a
> project of more closely identifying the town with the name of our
> national bard. He recognises Kilmarnock as the Mecca of Burns'
> lore, where the peerless poems were first published to the world,
> and where all literature associated with his honourable name has
> been carefully compiled and widely disseminated. Mr Carnegie has

therefore decided to erect, at his own cost, within the town of Kilmarnock, a temple to the memory of our national pride, provided the Council grant a free site. It is his intention to make this memorial a most elaborate one, the building to be constructed of granite, white marble, or some superior material, and to be of magnificent design, while the interior will contain statues of Burns' contemporaries and the principal characters of his creation, and, under the dome, a chaste figure of the immortal genius will stand. Artistic panels will embellish the walls, illustrative of scenes depicted in the poems, and the whole building will be lavishly created at a cost not exceeding £500,000. While Mr Carnegie will retain, in his own hands, the plans and details of the construction, he wishes the management of the Temple to be vested in a Committee of Trustees, consisting of the Provost, Magistrates and three of the people's representatives in the Council; the president, vice-president and other three members of the Kilmarnock Burns' Club; and the editor of the *Burns Chronicle*. In selecting a site, Mr Carnegie has confidence in the judgement of the Kilmarnock Town Council, but, when in Kilmarnock, he was impressed with a commanding position at the entrance of your park [Kay Park] opposite to Tam Samson's House, imposing flights of steps could be led up to the structure, and made add to the effect. Mr Carnegie will be glad to learn if the Kilmarnock Town Council are prepared to entertain the conditions of this gift, so that he can make the necessary arrangements for immediately proceeding therewith.

Yours faithfully, Hew Morrison (per J.C.)

The councillors sat quietly as the details in the letter were read to them, but all the while their bodies swelled with pride that someone as famous as Andrew Carnegie had decided that their town should be selected for the greatest memorial ever to Robert Burns – Kilmarnock before Alloway in Ayr, where he was born, or Dumfries where he died and was buried. Once the letter was read out the councillors quickly joined together in accepting the gift, and there was no real opposition to the location that Andrew Carnegie had selected himself. Provost Hood praised Carnegie for his wonderful gift, and Bailie [magistrate] Turnbull spoke in support, before the conditions of the gift were accepted.

That Carnegie knew Kilmarnock and was acquainted with the layout of the town was no surprise to the councillors, for the philanthropist had been in the town just the previous year. He had been invited to lay the foundation stone of the new Loanhead Elementary School on Saturday 29 August 1903, and on the same occasion he was presented with the freedom of the burgh. He was then entertained at a fine dinner in the town's George Hotel, and all was going exceedingly well until one council official dropped a hint to the great philanthropist that it would be an ideal time for him to make one of his announcements in which he could donate a considerable sum for the erection of a free library or museum. 'You have spoiled my day,' Carnegie responded, and the day was much more sombre from then on.

The letter that Provost Hood read out appeared to be genuine and the council took the offer of half a million pounds towards an international monument and library to Robert Burns very seriously. As soon as the council had agreed that the offer should be accepted, they lost no time in spreading the word. The local newspapers were made aware of the story, and soon national newspapers picked up the story and reported the offer.

However, within a few hours of the information being released to the press, the council discovered that the letter had been a hoax. *The Scotsman* was first to report back to the council, for they were quick to find Hew Morrison, who was Andrew Carnegie's representative in Scotland, and interview him. When Morrison denied writing the letter, or having any knowledge of Mr Carnegie's gift, the alarm bells began to ring. Hew Morrison stated categorically that if any letter had been sent to the council in Kilmarnock then an unwarranted use had been made of his name. Morrison reckoned that no such offer had been made from Andrew Carnegie, and considered that the philanthropist would 'be the last man in the world to think of perpetuating the memory of Burns in such an absurd memorial.' He confirmed that he had written no such letter, and that therefore the letter was not genuine.

Hew Morrison contacted Kilmarnock Burgh Council to offer them some support, writing:

Dear Provost Hood,

I offer you my sympathy in this wretched and silly hoax that has been perpetrated upon you, a hoax which I think not only silly, but insulting to the people of the town over which you so worthily preside. About 11:30 last night, Mr Gilbert of *The Scotsman* newspaper sent one of his men to ask me whether such a gift had really been given. That was the first I heard of it, and on learning from him that I was the supposed author of a letter read by yourself you may fancy my consternation. I at once repudiated the letter and characterised it as an impudent and cruel hoax. I tried to get into communication with yourself, but failed. I telephoned to ex-Provost Mackay, who was good enough to promise to communicate at once with you on the matter. I also communicated with the *Glasgow Herald* and the Press Association, London. I am very much distressed that such a trick should have been so far successful. What the object of the writer was may possibly come out some day. I do trust we shall be able to trace him, and the first step in that line will be for you to preserve the original letter, and submit it in the first instance to myself, so that I may see if anyone has had access to our stationery here, or where there has been any attempt to imitate my writing. I do feel very much for Mr Carnegie. The person who wrote the letter must have had an idea of Mr Carnegie's appreciation of his visit to your town, but the rest of the letter was not in any way characteristic of Mr Carnegie, and especially silly was the part regarding the structure and its composition.

The council was quickly summoned to a meeting on the morning of Thursday 11 February 1904. The gathering was a rather sombre one, not unlike people meeting with a hangover after a party the night before. The council accepted that they had been duped, and sent out letters and notices to as many papers as possible, advising them that they had been the victim of a great hoax, and that the press release issued just 24 hours earlier should be ignored.

The papers seized on the story with gusto. Instead of dropping the original announcement, they thought the story was now even better, and Kilmarnock's great hoax got the front page. Some even printed the public announcement of the gift, adding at the end that it had been discovered to be false. The local Ayrshire papers were soon filled with letters from readers threatening the hoaxer if he was caught.

The story spread quickly throughout the world. Instead of being a quiet but industrious Scottish town, the hoax connection with the world's richest philanthropist made it newsworthy. The *Boston News* ran the story in America, and many British newspapers reported the story. Some claimed that Kilmarnock had little humour, and had been an easy trick for the hoaxer, others thought that the council had been rather naïve in accepting the terms and publicly announcing them so quickly.

The council in Kilmarnock decided that they would need to do some investigating, to find out who the hoaxer was. The original letter was studied, and though it had been typewritten throughout, it had a printed heading claiming to be from 'The Public Free Library, George IV Bridge, Edinburgh'. The signature, 'Hew Morrison' was also typewritten, but someone had added the note 'per' and the initials 'J.C.' in ink.

The letter had been delivered to the town clerk's office on Wednesday morning, addressed to the Provost, the Town Hall, Kilmarnock.

The council passed the letter over to Captain George Hill, Chief Constable of Kilmarnock Burgh Police, and he confirmed very quickly that the letter was not written on paper used by the Free Library, and that therefore the letter heading had been especially printed for the hoax.

With a degree of sleuthing that would have put Sherlock Holmes in the shade, Captain Hill and his team began to search for the source of the letter. Typewriters around the town were checked to see if they produced similar typefaces. They didn't have far to go, for the typewriter in the police station was discovered to be the very one on which the letter had been typed. The type-writer was one that was usually used by Sergeant Martin, and he was quick to confirm that he had, indeed, been responsible for creating the letter. He had written it up between 9 p.m. and 10 p.m. one evening in January.

However, Sergeant Martin went on to state that he had written the letter at the request of a magistrate of the burgh, and as it was a magistrate that had asked him to do it, he neither questioned why such a letter should be written, or to what use it would be put.

The magistrate was identified by Sergeant Martin, and when approached by Captain Hill he confirmed that he had been responsible for directing the night officer in the police station to type the letter. Captain Hill reported back to Provost Hood, who was soon to receive confirmation from the perpetrator. In trying to bring the matter to a close, Provost Hood sent a press release to various newspapers:

I consider it my duty to intimate to the community that the gentleman who wrote the letter which was addressed to me and read at the last meeting of the Town Council has voluntarily admitted the authorship, and has accepted full responsibility for its production, to which I agree. He explains that the letter was not intended to become public property, and has expressed his sincere regret for his conduct. He has also handed me the sum of £50, which I have sent to the treasurer of the Infirmary; and I am confident that I express the general feeling when I say that I trust the very regrettable incident may now be considered at an end.

However, the public was not willing to let matters end so quickly. Rumours in the town claimed that it had been a prominent member of the town council who was responsible for ordering the writing of the letter, and the public felt that to allow him to remain anonymous was wrong.

On Friday 19 February a letter was presented to the provost, signed by nine members of the town council, requesting that he call a meeting at his earliest convenience to discuss matters concerning the whole hoax, and, if so resolved, to appoint a committee that would make inquiries into the whole circumstances of the incident, with powers to take the necessary action and report back on the case.

Another writer to the *Kilmarnock Standard* complained that this was 'too serious a matter' to let slip by, and the fact that the gentleman could afford £50 for the infirmary implied that 'there was one law for the rich and another for the poor.' What if it had been an ordinary working man? 'Civic' continued, 'I only express the hope that this "local gentleman" will show himself to be a gentleman and take the proper course to amend matters.'

Provost Hood acquiesced, and a special meeting of the council was held on Wednesday 24 February. Council meetings usually took place at 7 p.m., but this one was scheduled for 8 p.m. The public were aware of the meeting, and crowds gathered at the town hall from 6 p.m. onwards to discover the outcome. The press lined the corridors of the hall, meaning that the councillors had difficulty getting into the chamber. A number of journalists were too late to force their way into the town hall, but they were able to acquire a ladder and used it to reach a first-floor window, through which they entered the building. When all the councillors present had settled, the provost convened the meeting. Very soon he opened a letter and read its contents:

Howard Park,
Kilmarnock, Feby. 22, 1904.

Provost Hood, Kilmarnock,
Dear Sir,
As the author of the fictitious letter, purporting to have been sent
by Mr Hew Morrison on behalf of Dr Andrew Carnegie, I think
it due to you, to the Council, and to the community, as well as to
these gentlemen, that I should publicly accept entire and sole
responsibility for the production, and express my deep contrition.
I had no malicious intention in the matter, and did not expect or
desire that it should go so far; consequently I very much regret it
and hereby tender my sincere apology. As you are aware, I have
already made the 'amende honorable' [public confession] to Mr
Hew Morrison and also to yourself, as being more immediately
concerned, and at your request have contributed a sum to a charity
as some public reparation for my offence. I further have to intimate
that my resignation as a member of the Town Council will be
placed in the hands of the Clerk at the first ordinary meeting.
Believe me, yours most sincerely,
Wm. Munro.

It was noted that only two councillors were absent from the
meeting – Bailie William Munro and Matthew Robertson, who
was seriously unwell.

A second letter was then read out, written by George Hill of
Kilmarnock Police. In it he reported that he had received a letter
from Bailie William Munro, claiming all blame for the fictitious
letter, and requesting that Sergeant Martin should in no way be
blamed for any part in the hoax, as he had simply typed up the
letter at his request. Sergeant Martin, he noted, had been in the
police force for 24 years. During this time he had been a reliable
officer, and there had never been any blemish on his character.
Captain Hill had dealt with Sergeant Martin in the matter, and

taken steps to ensure that similar practices could not occur in the station again. He closed the letter by offering the council every assistance should they decide that the hoax must be the subject of any inquiry.

With Captain Hill's letter was the original letter sent to him by Bailie Munro. In it he apologised for having involved Sergeant Martin in the proceedings, but informed Captain Hill that Martin, 'knew nothing whatever as to the purpose to which it was to be put, I trust you will bear this fact in mind in dealing with him, I should be exceedingly sorry if he was made to suffer for an offence which is entirely mine.'

The council discussed the letters and their contents for some time, and deliberated on what the next course of action should be. It was eventually decided that the matter should be remitted to the Watching and Lighting Committee and that they should make enquiries and report back.

Bailie William Munro, who had admitted his guilt in writing the letter, had been a man of some standing in the town. He had been a councillor for nine years, and was serving his second term as a magistrate (known in Scotland as a bailie). Only in January 1904 had he been appointed as a justice of the peace. He was also one of those named in the freedom of the burgh document that had been presented to Andrew Carnegie the previous year. The papers reported that he had been involved in many benevolent works and that he had given excellent service as the secretary of the newly created rifle range in the town. Munro was also a prominent businessman, being a partner in the preserve and jam-making company known as Gilmour & Smith, located at Low Glencairn Street. It was quite ironic that the trademark used by the company was none other than a sketch of the town's Burns Monument. The company produced 'jams, jellies and marmalade which are made from the richest fruit and pure cane sugar', and won the 'highest award for marmalade at the Edinburgh International Exhibition, 1886'.

The town council again discussed the Burns Temple hoax at their meeting on Wednesday 9 March 1904. The Watching and Lighting Committee reported back. They confirmed that Bailie Munro's claim to have been the sole perpetrator of the hoax was correct, and that Sergeant Martin had indeed written the letter at Munro's request. No other police officer was aware that the letter had been written or had any part in its composition. The committee also reported that they were satisfied with the way Sergeant Martin had been dealt with by his superiors.

Provost Hood thanked the committee for their report, and hoped that this would bring the whole sorry event to a conclusion. Bailie Turnbull moved that the report should be adopted, which was agreed. It was also agreed that all references to the Burns Temple letter and its ramifications should be expunged from the minutes of the council.

The people of Kilmarnock would not let the story lie, however. One enterprising stationer, Mrs Tommy Rodger of 126 King Street, had a number of cartoon postcards issued celebrating the hoax. One of these depicted a new Kilmarnock tram (yet to be officially opened) making its way to 'Burns Temple and Tam Samson's Hoose.' The tram was crammed full of dignitaries in top hats and outside the large Grecian-styled temple stood statues to Provost Hood and Bailie Munro. Another postcard showed Bailie Munro on his knees, handing over his £50 donation to the Kilmarnock Infirmary.

The author of *The Humours of Ayrshire* (*c.*1880-1900), John Aitken, produced a small chapbook a few years after the hoax, entitled *A Lost Half Million: Story of the Burns Temple Hoax*.

The resignation of Munro resulted in a by-election for the fifth ward in Kilmarnock, which covered the Glencairn part of the town. This took place in April 1904, at which John Carnie was elected.

Bailie Munro lay low for some time. He was known in the town as ex-Bailie Munro, and it was quite a few months before he showed his face at any public event. However, in June, he attended a lecture in the town on the Lost Tribes of Israel, his attendance being significant enough for the *Kilmarnock Standard* to report it. The other local paper, the *Kilmarnock Herald*, reported that he had been busily involved in organising the annual trip for the Howard Park Old Men's Cabin to the coast at Troon.

Council elections took place on 1 November 1904. Ex-Bailie Munro threw his hat into the ring, offering himself as a candidate for his old seat. At a meeting in the Riccarton Institute he addressed the audience:

> I am here at your request to thank you for letting me have my say in certain matters that have affected Kilmarnock, or, rather, have wounded those who profess to uphold the dignity of our town, but who have yet to learn how to conduct themselves in dignity. I have never ceased to consider myself your representative . . . I don't claim to be above the average in wisdom, and would never think of advocating that the Council should be composed of twenty-five Bailie Munros. But I am sure you will agree with me that, if it were so constituted, more business would be transacted and there would be less nonsense than there has been these last number of years.

Bailie Munro came first in the election, returning to the same council seat that he was forced into resigning less than eight months earlier. With a degree of irony that was noted at the time, William Munro not only was returned to the council, but he was appointed as dean of guild, a position of some authority in the town. Even later, the great hoaxer was honoured with a street named after him, Munro Avenue being a significant road on the west side of the town.

# 5

## *The Highland Famine Fiddle: Alexander Bannatyne*

In the middle of the nineteenth century there was a serious famine throughout much of Scotland. There had been a number of bad summers during the 1840s and this was followed by a major outbreak of potato blight. This decimated much of the crop, leaving families with little food to survive the winter months. With practically no hope of alternative employment, many thousands of Highlanders were left starving.

*The Inverness Courier* of 26 August 1846 reported:

> It is truly lamentable to witness the fearful ravages of the potato rot in the island of Lews [Lewis], and still more melancholy to contemplate the sad consequences to the poor during the next twelve months, many of whom are already representing themselves as in a starving condition.

Eventually the plight of the Highlanders reached the corridors of power, and parliament in London felt that it would have to act. Accordingly, in 1846 the sum of £20,000 was allocated by parliament for a relief fund for the starving Highlanders.

In February 1847 the central committee of the Highland

Destitution Relief Board and Committee was established to oversee the work of various local fundraising boards. In Glasgow one of the local boards had been formed earlier; the first chairman was Alexander Hastie, Lord Provost of Glasgow, the secretary was Charles Baird. This committee was charged with organising the distribution of the foodstuffs to the starving Highlanders, as well as with raising funds for the purchase of more supplies. By the end of 1847 the board had raised over £200,000, thought to be the largest single cash sum raised in Scotland during the nineteenth century for the relief of distress (T. M. Devine, *The Great Highland Famine*, 1988).

The first official meeting of the Glasgow Relief Committee took place on 12 January 1847 in the Merchants' Hall, on Glasgow's Hutcheson Street. One of the speakers who addressed the meeting was Rev. Dr Norman MacLeod, who explained the scale of the problem:

> If we take the population suffering from the failure of the potato crop at around 300,000, and taking five as the average of every family, we shall have 60,000 families requiring a supply for keeping them in existence for eight months, till relief comes with the next harvest. The lowest calculation that we can make is at the rate of two and a half stones of meal per week to every family, a requirement of 75,000 sacks of meal per month, or 600,000 sacks for the eight months. At the present rate of thirty shillings per sack, the total cost would be in the region of £1,000,000.

It was decided that tenders would be sought from grain dealers in the central lowlands for the supply of oatmeal and barley. Applications to tender were sent out to many dealers, and a number of these responded with quotes.

One of the suppliers who tendered was Alexander Bannatyne, based in Glasgow's Hope Street. He had been in business in the city for some time, and his reputation was good. A delegation from the Relief Committee paid a visit to his stores and sampled his grain, which was found to be of a suitable quality. As a result of the price tendered, and the standard of his produce, the first contract was awarded to Bannatyne.

The first load of barley and meal left Glasgow's Broomielaw on board the steamer *Aurora*. One thousand sacks had been loaded onto the boat and it set sail for the West Highlands. The delivery of the grain was eagerly anticipated by the starving Highlanders, and it was successfully distributed amongst the needy families. Further shipments took place each day, and soon Bannatyne was able to send off his invoice for the first part of the contract. This was worth £11,000, around £800,000 in today's figures.

However, Bannatyne became greedy and started to tamper with the grain that he was sending north. The first public notice of this occurred in February 1847 when a letter was sent to Peter MacKenzie, the editor of the *Reformers Gazette*. MacKenzie was one of Glasgow's most respected citizens, having been an advocate and founder of the *Gazette*. The letter had been sent by one Alexander Lauder, and in it he claimed that he had proof that the grain being sent north by Bannatyne was unfit for human consumption. Although the grain sampled by the Relief Committee's men was of the best quality, the grain that was being sent to feed the Highlanders was mixed with other substances, including sawdust and animal feed.

At the time MacKenzie dismissed the letter, thinking it may have been written by someone who bore a grudge against Bannatyne and was trying to damage his reputation. However, a week later a second letter arrived, again from Lauder, in which he suggested that MacKenzie join him in a night-time observation of Bannatyne's meal stores, when proof of the claim could be substantiated.

Intrigued, MacKenzie decided to go. He met Lauder and another man at the foot of the city's Union Street just around midnight. They walked up the street to the Unitarian Church building, which had a number of large vaults beneath the floor of the nave. These were let to various merchants and were used as storerooms. The three men stood at the door at the side of the church for a few minutes. Soon someone unlocked the door from within and quietly beckoned them inside.

In silence, MacKenzie and the two men walked along some passageways to one of the vaults. Within, barely visible in the dim light, they could see hundreds of sacks of oatmeal, piled against the walls of the chamber. In the middle even more sacks were piled high. The meal in these sacks was of a high quality. However, MacKenzie was then led to another door, through which he was allowed to peek.

Within the building the sight that greeted him left him speechless. However, he was later able to recount:

Such a sight! Dozens of men and boys – 'dusty millers' they were called – were seen with dirty white nightcaps on their heads, and others with masks on their faces and over their mouths, obviously to prevent the dust from choking them; while others, with shovels and rakes, were turning over the meal ingredients – one shovelful of good meal with two or three of the adulterated stuff – and filling the first thousand bags as quickly as they could do for shipment at the Broomielaw. It was a most suffocating sight – the stour and the stuff and the villainous ingredients had a direct tendency almost to choke the breath; but there was liquor aplenty to clear the throat, and stimulate the arms of those engaged at the work. For every ten bags made up for the Highland Relief Committee they got a good caulker of Highland whisky, with plenty of porter and ale, bread and cheese, to encourage them on throughout the night; for this was night-work, dark night-work in reality. I soon saw sufficient reason to satisfy me that the representation originally made to me by Mr Lauder was too true – too glaring, too infamous, wicked and abominable.

In great excitement, Lauder and MacKenzie called on the offices of the Highland Relief Committee and informed them of the disclosure. The reception was less than welcome, the committee representatives present disbelieving them, and claiming that nothing could be done for at least four days, the time it would take to get the full committee together for an emergency meeting. MacKenzie and Lauder suggested that Bannatyne should be approached for an explanation, or even that he and his workers should be arrested by the police, but these comments were ignored by the committee.

Frustrated by the lack of action, MacKenzie and Lauder decided to bide their time until the next meeting of the committee. However, before this took place, they were to receive more evidence of the fraud being carried out by Bannatyne.

Apparently, word reached Bannatyne that there was some doubt about the quality of the grain he was sending to the Highlands. He decided to ensure that he was not caught, and that his night workers were loyal to him. He informed them that he was now doubling their wages, but that they would have to work constantly for the following 48 hours in order to mix the grain with the sawdust and cattle-feed, as well as transport it to the Broomielaw, ready for passage up the west coast of Scotland. So keen were the workers at the doubling of their wages that they managed to complete the work within 36 hours.

Lauder, MacKenzie, and one member of the Relief Committee, made their way early in the morning to the Clyde at Broomielaw. It was the day that the steamer was due to be loaded with Bannatyne's cargo. They gained access to the storage sheds, and within found the sacks that had been delivered there from Bannatyne's stores. One of these had been ripped during transport and placed aside. The men gathered some of the grain from the sack and made a hasty exit before they were seen.

The grain that had been gathered in the storage sheds was sent to Dr Penny, who worked at the Andersonian Institute, at the University of Strathclyde. He examined the grain and was able to determine that it consisted of some oatmeal of human standard adulterated with low-quality oatmeal, normally used for feeding horses, and some sawdust.

With confirmation that the oatmeal had been tampered with in order to boost Bannatyne's profits, the Relief Committee quickly met. It was too late to stop Bannatyne's cargo from being loaded onto the steamer, and as it was now sailing for the western seaboard of Scotland, Bannatyne thought that he was safe. The committee, however, decided it would have to get incontrovertible proof and so made arrangements for six men to travel to various ports in the west of Scotland where Bannatyne's grain was due to arrive. Accordingly, two men were sent to Portree on Skye, two to Tobermory on Mull, and two to Oban in Argyll.

When the boats arrived at the ports, the men were to inform the distributors that the unloading of the grain should be halted. They also sampled one-in-twenty sacks, and packets of grain were taken from these sacks back to Glasgow for analysis. Again, Dr Penny carried this out at the university, and he discovered that each sack contained a mixture similar to the grain that had been taken from the Broomielaw stores.

The Relief Committee summoned Bannatyne to appear before its meeting in March 1847. The grain was shown to him, and the evidence of Dr Penny was presented. Bannatyne listened to the accusations being made, and when the committee had finished he told them that they were wrong, and that all the grain that he supplied had been of the quality specified in the original contract. He then went further, threatening to sue the Relief Committee for defamation of character.

The committee then produced letters signed by a number of Bannatyne's own workers in which they confirmed that they had been asked to blend the meal with other substances. On seeing this, Bannatyne rose from the meeting and with his legal adviser stormed from the room.

With Bannatyne's reaction indicative of his guilt, the Relief

Committee decided to pass all the evidence over to George Salmond, the Procurator Fiscal. He issued a warrant for the arrest of Bannatyne. When he appeared in custody his particulars were taken and he was released on bail within a few hours.

When word of Bannatyne's fraud spread throughout the city it resulted in a public outcry. Bannatyne, however, spent the following six months trying to clear his name. He also attempted to prevent witnesses from testifying against him. He contacted Lauder and offered him the chance to start a new life in America – he would pay for a one-way ticket and give him a substantial amount of cash to set himself up in business. Lauder refused the bribe. His night-workers were all given large payouts to keep quiet, and most of them were offered work in England, where they would be given better jobs which paid substantially more.

Alexander Bannatyne was tried in the Glasgow Court of Justiciary on Wednesday 29 September 1847. He was accused of 'falsehood, fraud and wilful imposition.' The witnesses told of their visit to the Unitarian Church, the sample taken from the Broomielaw and of the samples acquired from the sacks at the ports in the west of Scotland. In his defence, Bannatyne claimed that it was normal for grain merchants to mix high-quality grain with what was known as 'thirds', as the high quality grain was often too rich for consumption, and that by reducing its quality it became what he called 'more wholesome'.

The Lord Justice Clerk summed up the full-day's hearing by pointing out that:

> What you have to consider is whether oatmeal – an article much used by the lower classes of this country – could, in an onerous transaction of sale, be anything other than oatmeal. Whether there is one tittle of evidence which went to show that the Committee had ever manifested a desire to obtain a cheap article, or that they wanted any article whatsoever but oatmeal.

The trial concluded at quarter to eleven at night, and the jury took just 20 minutes to decide that Bannatyne was guilty. On the morning of Friday 1 November 1847 Bannatyne was sentenced to four months in gaol, in addition to a fine of £400. The sentence was seen by many throughout Scotland as too lenient, but their outrage was to be greater a few weeks later when it was announced that Bannatyne was to be released from gaol and his sentence quashed. Apparently, in the meantime, a number of his influential friends had been at work, persuading those in authority that Bannatyne should be freed. A few weeks later it was quietly announced by the Secretary of State for Scotland that he would not be required to pay his fine either.

# 6

# The Military Hero: 'Sir' Alan McIlwraith

The publication of Scotland's new celebrity magazine, *No. 1*, in 2006 caused quite a stir. On the cover were the usual images of Scottish celebrities and there were articles on fashion and lifestyles within the pages. However, the magazine also specialised in photographs of ladies and gentlemen attending charity balls, awards nights and premieres, and it was one of these that considerably raised the profile of the new magazine.

Included amongst the photographs of the 'Women of Influence' award ceremony, held in Glasgow's Barony Halls, was one of Lady Shona and Sir Alan McIlwraith. The ceremony was arranged by the National Children's Homes charity, and in the picture Sir Alan was dressed in full military regalia, complete with medals.

However, 'Sir' Alan McIlwraith was a complete fake. He was nothing more than plain Alan McIlwraith, a 28-year-old man who worked at a computer manufacturer's call centre, earning £16,000 per annum.

McIlwraith had always been interested in the army, and through time had started collecting bits of army gear. Eventually, using the internet on-line auction company Ebay, he was able to buy almost all the relevant pieces of uniform and medals to convince others of his military credentials. He claimed that he was a war hero, and that for his various acts of bravery he had been given numerous awards. These included a knighthood in 2005 (a Knight of the British Empire, according to him), the Distinguished Service Order (DSO), and the Military Cross.

McIlwraith told of his heroic exploits serving his country in Afghanistan, Sierra Leone, Northern Ireland and Kosovo. He even made up his military education, claiming that he was trained at Sandhurst Military Academy, where he came top in his class. Previously, he was supposed to have studied at Glasgow University, but they were later to confirm that he had never studied there. Following Sandhurst he was supposed to have become second-in-command of the 2nd Parachute Regiment, with which he served in Northern Ireland. So gifted was he, or so he claimed, that he acted as an adviser to General Wesley Clark, the Supreme Allied Commander of NATO in Europe.

Other tales recounted by McIlwraith included one in which he was responsible for saving the life of a young woman. Apparently a riotous mob was about to attack the woman. McIlwraith, at least in his mind, rode in on his charger and saved her life, totally unarmed. It may have been for this act of selfless bravery that he was supposed to have been knighted.

When it was revealed that the soldier and his 'wife' in *No. 1*'s photo gallery were frauds, the media pounced on the story. Investigative journalists contacted all the organisations McIlwraith claimed he was connected with to find out more. The National Children's Homes charity, the organisers of the fund-raising ball, reported, 'we are looking into the circumstances of his involvement with the charity as a matter of urgency.' How McIlwraith managed to get an invitation was investigated.

He had also managed to book tickets to other charity events, sometimes asking his girlfriend, Shona McLaughlan, to do it. On one occasion she claimed that she was personal assistant to 'Major

Sir Alan McIlwraith', and ordered tickets for the £60-a-head Wags [comedians] Dinner at Glasgow's prestigious Marriott Hotel, which raises funds for Epilepsy Scotland. Alan had previously emailed the charity to ask the price of the tickets. Shona paid for the tickets using her mother's credit card. Shona asked the organiser what the dress code was, and when she was informed that it was a black tie event, she told them that 'Sir' Alan would probably wear his mess uniform. When he was revealed as a fraud the organisers reckoned 'Sir' Alan would not have the nerve to show his face.

Buckingham Palace officials were asked if there was any chance that he had received a knighthood, but they were able to confirm that they had no record of him being honoured in this way, or of receiving the DSO.

The army was contacted and responded that no Alan McIlwraith had been given the Military Cross. From studying the picture they could confirm that the uniform was a mish-mash of different uniforms, and that he wore it rather untidily. The army spokesman stated:

He is incorrectly dressed, and his medals and honours are fraudulent. The minute I saw the state of his uniform I knew that he was a fraud. His uniform is two sizes too big for him and his medals are mounted all squint. On the Royal Highland Fusiliers uniform he has three pips on the epaulette which denotes a captain. On the Parachute Regiment uniform he has a crown on his epaulette which means he has promoted himself to major. His claims are ridiculous, but also quite serious because they are an insult to those who have earned these awards through their own merit. He's never even been in the Territorial Army; he's never even been in the army cadets. It doesn't sound like he's the full shilling.

McIlwraith was keen to promote himself in his military hero guise, and even went to the length of creating his own page in the online internet encyclopaedia, *Wikipedia*. He submitted his first article on 5 October 2005 under the username 'MilitaryPro.' In the encyclopaedia, in which users can create new entries which can be added to or edited by others, McIlwraith claimed that he 'is known throughout the military world as a man that can get things done, and is thought of as a hero that the UK and NATO can look to in times of trouble.' Another quote was supposedly by General Sir Mike Jackson, head of the army, who stated that 'Very few photographs of Captain McIlwraith are in circulation as he is camera-shy, but a splendid soldier. He's best known for risking his life to protect his men. For this he was awarded the DSO.' Readers of Wikipedia nominated the page as a suspected hoax on 10 October 2005, just five days after it had been posted, and by 26 October it had been deleted. Wikipedia, which has a vetting system for preventing fraudulent entries, had removed it. However, 'Sir' Alan resubmitted it a number of times, and each time it was deleted.

Alan McIlwraith started a new job at the Dell Computer Corporation call centre in Glasgow's City Park business park in January 2006, answering calls from businesses requesting quotes for repairs to office computers. Previously he worked for a competing computer company. At his desk in the call centre he had a nameplate with his name engraved as 'Sir Alan McIlwraith' and the same name was embossed on his gold credit card, though both these claims were later denied. On the wall in the call centre was a print-out of his Wikipedia submission, perhaps more to remind him of what he had been telling others, than to impress his colleagues. Alongside it was a picture of him in his Royal Highland Fusiliers uniform. Many of his colleagues didn't really believe that he was a knight, or that he was a military hero in demand by charities, even though he often turned up for work dressed in his army uniform, claiming that he had to leave work and head off directly to various functions.

A few colleagues looked up the internet to find out about

McIlwraith's knighthood, and discovered that it did not seem to exist. He was to explain this away by claiming that he had requested its removal as he did not wish to attract publicity. Other tales that he recounted to workmates included the fact that he had been involved in negotiations over the merging of the various Scottish army regiments, an event that was very contentious and high-profile at the time. On the day that the regiments were formally united at a ceremony held at Edinburgh Castle, McIlwraith turned up rather late for work dressed in a long Crombie coat, his suit underneath, and a pair of army boots. He told his workmates that he had been at an army meeting at which they had all been given a bottle of wine and a box of Quality Street chocolates. To prove it, he had brought the box of chocolates to work to share out.

Sir Alan's claims were recounted by colleagues when they were questioned by national newspapers. One related that McIlwraith claimed to have killed several people during his spell on active service. He also was outspoken in his condemnation of Americans, due to them not adhering to the Geneva Convention on human rights.

Colleagues at the call centre reported that McIlwraith was delighted with his image, and when *No. 1* magazine published a picture of him and his girlfriend, he brought in a copy of the magazine and showed it around. He claimed that National Children's Homes wished him to attend more of their functions, and that he was also getting involved with cancer and epilepsy charities.

A workmate reported to a newspaper that:

McIlwraith tells everyone he is a war hero and a sir. He goes to work in army boots, khaki socks and a suit and tie. He says he is better that Sir Sean Connery because he gained his knighthood from army service. At first we thought it was a bit funny because he doesn't look like he could fight his way out of a wet paper bag.

He has just gone too far. He's an insult to anyone who has ever served in the armed forces. We don't know whether his girlfriend is aware he's a fraud or if, like so many people, she has been duped.

McIlwraith's girlfriend was probably duped as well. Colleagues at her work, where she was an insurance underwriter, claimed that she had always been interested in military life and that her father had been a sergeant with the military police. She had tried to join the RAF in 2004, but was not accepted, claiming that this was down to either her height or weight. When his tale was exposed McIlwraith attempted suicide. Shona took him to hospital and left him there, later sending him his engagement ring back by post, not even including a message.

When the Scottish newspaper the *Daily Record* interviewed McIlwraith he was still adamant that he was telling the truth. Explaining the difference in his ranks, he claimed that he had only recently been promoted to the rank of major. His knighthood had been granted 'for services to the Crown', and he claimed that Prince Charles had performed the ceremony. The reporter from the newspaper informed him that investigations with the army and Buckingham Palace had produced no record of him, to which he responded, 'I'm in the SAS, that's why it won't be on record.'

McIlwraith lived at home with his mother, father and younger brother. His mother had no idea of his fantasies, and when she discovered what he was doing she was heartbroken. He eventually admitted to his made-up life, saying 'I have not got the education to be an officer in the army. I have not got the build to be anything to do with the army. I have not got the co-ordination. Everything that you need to be an officer in the army I have probably not got.'

Alan claimed that the whole episode began when he was hit over the head with a piece of scaffolding by some youths in the street. He had been bullied for much of his life, due to his small stature and thin body, and he reckoned that if he could create a superhero alter-ego then this would deter bullying. If he could portray himself as being better than he was, then he reckoned people would either leave him alone, or even look up to him. He struck upon the idea of becoming an army hero after watching a television programme. He then read everything he could about the army and started buying medals and uniform on the internet.

Relating his story to a newspaper reporter, McIlwraith went on:

> The lie had just gone too deep. It's like a weed that invades your life. Once it has taken root there is nothing that you can do about it. It's like a game of Buckaroo, everybody keeps adding something on and you have got to try to keep up with everything. My mind started going like, 'this is who you are,' and this is when I started thinking that it was true. I believed that I had been to all these places. The doctors say it stemmed from when I got smacked on the head. My mind went loopy.

'Last year was probably the best year of my life,' said McIlwraith. 'I had a good job, I met Shona, and went to Egypt on holiday. This year has been the worst of my life.' McIlwraith lost his job, his fiancée and many of his friends. He saw little hope for the future, thinking it unlikely that he would get another job or girlfriend, aware of the fact that many people disliked him.

'Sir' Alan McIlwraith managed to make his name, however. He has been restored as an entry in Wikipedia, but he is now listed in the encyclopaedia as a fraud. In the new entry the original article has been reproduced, as well as a photograph depicting Sir Alan in his army uniform, his chest bedecked with medals.

# 7

# *The Prince of Poyais:*
# *Sir Gregor MacGregor*

One of the greatest fraudsters in the history of Scotland was Gregor MacGregor. So elaborate were his frauds that they destroyed people's lives – all with the aim of making MacGregor a fortune and allowing him to live his lifestyle of choice.

Gregor MacGregor was born in Edinburgh on Christmas Eve 1786, in a grand Georgian town house in the capital's Queen Street. He had a decent upbringing, for he was connected to a number of notable Scots families, and was able to live in the best of houses. Whilst still an infant of ten months, he was left in the care of a drunken nurse and his foot was burned in an accident. The family were rich enough to enjoy holidays at various times, staying on relative's estates and even travelling as far as France. The MacGregors were descendants of Clan Dughaill Ciar, as the MacGregors of Glengyle were known in Gaelic. Accordingly, Gregor MacGregor could count Rob Roy MacGregor and numerous other clan heroes as relations. His grandfather, Gregor *Boidheach* MacGregor, is famed in MacGregor clan histories as 'Gregor the Beautiful', hero of various military battles, and the person who persuaded the government to repeal the Act of Proscription (an act banning membership of

Clan Gregor, dating from 1603) against the MacGregors in 1774.

At the age of ten, Gregor inherited his grandfather's property at Inverardrine, a small lairdship that lies in Glen Dochart, to the east of Crianlarich. Today it is little more than a house, its lands being afforested, located at the foot of a glen that drains the slopes of Cruach Ardrain and Stob Garbh. Modern maps spell it as Inverardran. Inverardran was part of the extensive estates of the Earl of Perth, though these were forfeited after the Jacobite Rising of 1745. The farm was feued to Gregor MacGregor Drummond in 1775, and in 1796 it became the property of Gregor MacGregor, the great fraudster. He was later to sell the ten acres of land – which was all the ancestral estate amounted to! – to Alexander MacNichol in 1828.

Gregor was educated in Edinburgh, firstly at Laing's Academy, followed by Taylor's Boarding School in Musselburgh, which he left at the age of 14. Soon after this Gregor enlisted in the army, serving with the 57th Regiment as an ensign in 1803. By 1805 he had been promoted to the rank of captain, but in 1810 he disagreed with some of his army superiors and either left or was forced out of the regiment. He then enlisted in the 8th Line Battalion of the Portuguese army, serving in the Peninsular Wars. He may have transferred to the Spanish army, for it is claimed that he was knighted by the Spanish king for his military service. Certainly, he later claimed to be Sir Gregor MacGregor, and supposedly was given permission by King George IV to use his Spanish title in Britain.

He met and married Maria Bowater, daughter of the late Admiral Bowater, in 1805, at the age of 18. She was often left behind when Gregor served in the army, but they spent some time together in London, Edinburgh and on the Isle of Wight. However, she died in 1811 just before they were ready to sail to Venezuela, MacGregor having decided to join Simón Bolívar, the liberator of Latin America, in his campaign against the oppressive

Spaniards. Apparently, MacGregor was keen to make his name in military circles, and to be spoken of in awe, like his grandfather, Gregor *Boidheach* MacGregor.

MacGregor journeyed to South America where he served against the Spanish. He met Doña Josefa Antonia Andrea Lovera, Simón Bolívar's niece. Josefa, as she was known, was something of a beauty, and she was already engaged to an officer. However, she was won over by Gregor and it was not unknown for her to accompany MacGregor into battle, where she could fight like any man. They were married at the Maracay Barracks on 12 June 1812, Bolívar giving the couple his blessing. Josefa, known as Lady MacGregor, had her portrait painted in 1824 by Charles Lees, now preserved in the National Portrait Gallery in London. Gregor and Josefa had three children, Gregorio, Josefa and Constantino.

In Venezuela, MacGregor was appointed a colonel under General Francisco de Miranda. He impressed the great leader and was quickly raised to brigadier, leading his men into battle at Los Guayos and elsewhere. However, a major earthquake in 1812 destroyed Caracas and district, resulting in MacGregor losing much of his property. General Miranda was captured when his army was defeated, but MacGregor managed to escape, making his way to Jamaica. For a number of years he took part in various army campaigns in the Caribbean, but eventually went back to Venezuela, where he was appointed colonel once more, under Simón Bolívar, who regarded him as one of the world's most skilful military leaders.

MacGregor was a major figure in the Venezuelan War of Independence, leading his men in significant events such as the siege of Cartagena in 1815, the battles of Maracay, La Victoria, San Sebástian de Los Reyes and Quebrada Honda. For his part he was awarded the Order of Libertadores, the highest honour that he could be given by the government. He continued to fight after Bolívar was defeated at Ocumare in 1816, and is regarded as a hero in Venezuela.

In 1817 Gregor MacGregor was given the authority of various people from Mexico, Rio de la Plata (Buenos Aires), New Grenada and Venezuela to attempt to take Amelia Island. This island lies on the east coast of America, on the boundary between Georgia and Florida. At the time Florida was under Spanish control and the United States wanted to add it to its list of states, but previous attempts at buying the land from Spain had failed, and for political reasons the US did not want to invade the territory. MacGregor was seen as a suitable person to take the island unofficially, and after this had been done it was hoped that the locals would come out in support and opt to join America.

On 29 June 1817 MacGregor led a band of 73 men onto the island and attacked the Spanish garrison there. The Spanish were caught by surprise so only one shot was fired, and this was in error. The island was taken and the 'Green Cross' of Florida, a flag with a white field and a green cross, similar in layout to St George's Cross, was hoisted. Soon a proclamation was issued:

### PROCLAMATION
of the Liberating Army

Gregor MacGregor, Brigadier General of the armies of the United Provinces of New Grenada and Venezuela, and general in chief of the armies for the two Floridas, commissioned by the Supreme Director of Mexico, South America, &c.

To the inhabitants of the Island of Amelia:

Your brethren of Mexico, Buenos Aries, New Grenada and Venezuela, who are so gloriously engaged in fighting for that inestimable gift which nature has bestowed upon her children, and which all civilized nations have endeavoured to secure by social compact – desirous that all the sons of Columbia should participate in the imprescriptable right – have confided to me the command of the land and naval forces.

Peaceable inhabitants of Amelia! Do not apprehend any danger or oppression from the troops which are now in possession of your Island, either for your persons, property or religion. However various the climes in which they may have received their birth, they are nevertheless your brethren and friends. Their first object will be to protect your rights; your property will be held sacred and inviolable; and every thing done to promote your real interests, by cooperating with you in carrying into effect the virtuous desires of our constituents; thereby becoming the instruments for the commencement of a national emancipation. Unite your forces with ours until America shall be plated with her high destinies to that rank among the nations that the Most High has appointed. A country by its extent and fertility offering the greatest sources of wealth and happiness.

The moment is important! Let it not escape without having commenced the great work of delivering Columbia from that tyranny which has been exercised in all parts; and which, to continue its power, has kept the people in the most degrading ignorance depriving them of the advantages resulting from a free intercourse with other nations; and of that prosperity which the arts and sciences produce when under the protection of wholesome laws, which you will be enabled properly to appreciate, only when you will have become a free people.

You who, ill-advised, have abandoned your homes, whatever may be the place of your birth, your political or religious opinions, return without delay, and resume your wonted occupations. Deprecate the evil counsels your enemies may disseminate among you. Listen to the voice of honour! To the promises of a sincere and disinterested friend, and return to the fulfilment of those duties which nature has imposed on you. He, who will not swear to maintain that independence which has been declared, will be allowed six months to settle his affairs, or to sell or remove his property without molestation, and enjoy all the advantages which the laws grant in such cases.

Friends, or enemies of our present system of emancipation, whoever you be, what I say unto you is the language of truth; it is the only language becoming a man of honour, and as such I swear to adhere, religiously to the tenor of this proclamation.

Dated at headquarters, Amelia Island, June 30th, 1817.

GREGOR MAC GREGOR

Jph. de Yribarren, Secretary

MacGregor took control of the island, establishing within a short period of time his own post office and court. The island was a popular port with pirates and privateers and MacGregor encouraged them to land, charging them a tax based on what they had plundered. He also produced a commemorative medal, on one side of which was inscribed 'Liberty for all the Floridas under the leadership of MacGregor' – obviously hoping for greater things to come.

MacGregor was quick to produce his own banknotes, which were used to pay his soldiers, even though the notes were basically worthless. He also printed 'scripts' which were certificates granting 2,000 acres of Florida land to the purchaser at a cost of $1,000, failing which they would be refunded with interest. It is known that MacGregor managed to raise $160,000 by issuing these certificates, and this scam set him planning a larger fraud.

However, the Spanish forces were regrouping, and were later to attack Amelia Island from their larger garrison at St Augustine, 50 miles to the south. MacGregor's smaller force held out for a short time before they were forced to flee by boat to the Bahamas. MacGregor had been half promised support from America once he had taken Amelia Island, but this was never to come.

MacGregor returned to Britain and gathered a further force of men, intending to sail back to Central America, where he planned to fight for Simón Bolívar in Panama. However, as he sailed with his four vessels, there was a mutiny, and MacGregor was left with a smaller force. He took the island of San Andreas and declared it for Colombia. As a result he was honoured with the title 'El MacGregor.' He then took San Jeronimo and San Fernando in Panama but again was forced out when Spain retaliated. For three years MacGregor lived the life of a pirate in the Caribbean, attacking ships and various Spanish forts along the coast.

MacGregor's experience on Amelia Island in granting fraudulent bonds for land that was never his gave him the idea for his greatest fraud. To the north and west of San Andreas Island lies what was a swampy and undeveloped stretch of country, known as the Costa de Mosquitos, or the Mosquito Coast. This wasn't named after the mosquito insects, but the Miskito Indians who had an independent country there, now on the borders between Nicaragua and Honduras. The 'king' – he was never really a king, but the ruler of the country – George Frederic Augustus, and Gregor MacGregor became friends for a time.

One night in April 1820, when MacGregor was plying George with the finest Scotch whisky and Caribbean rum that he had, he persuaded him to grant MacGregor the titles to around 8 million acres (or around 12,500 square miles) of this swampy territory. The grant was indefinite, and MacGregor now found himself the new chief, or Cazique in the local language, of a territory extending from the Caribbean shores inland to the high mountains of Cordillera Isabelia. King George Frederic Augustus was later to regret granting the land to MacGregor, but he did not command much respect in the country at the time, and no doubt he felt that by bringing in a strong leader to work under him he would be able to maintain greater control.

With the grant of land confirmed, MacGregor and Josefa set sail for Britain. MacGregor had plenty of time to hatch his plan, which was to sell farms and estates on the territory to British nationals, who would develop the infrastructure and, 'protected by the wise and vigorous administration, sound policy, and comprehensive view of His Highness the Cazique of Poyais, this beautiful country will rapidly advance in prosperity and civilization, and will become, in every point of view, and within a very short period, not the least considerable of those "radiant realms beyond the Atlantic wave"'. He produced a book all about the country, entitled *Sketch of the Mosquito Shore, including the Territory of Poyais, descriptive of the country*, and this was eventually published in Edinburgh by William Blackwood in 1822. Purportedly written by Captain Thomas Strangeways, it is thought that this wonderful account, with its glowing descriptions of how the new settler would flourish, was in fact written by MacGregor himself, based on an earlier account of Central America. In the publication he explained how a small grant of land would allow a settler to make a massive profit from natural resources.

In London in 1820, MacGregor informed the authorities that he was Gregor I, chief of Poyais, a name he had created. He was fêted by the authorities, the Lord Mayor of London, Christopher Magnay, organising a special reception in the Guild Hall on his behalf.

MacGregor began to raise money in Britain that was supposed to assist in the creation of the infrastructure of the country. He issued 2,000 bearer bonds worth £100 each on 23 October 1822 through the London Royal Exchange. He also had elaborate certificates printed, Poyaisian Landgrants, which were for various sizes of holdings of the finest and most productive countryside in the world. In his promotional material, MacGregor claimed that Poyais had its own public buildings, banks, cathedrals, opera houses, and the usual trappings of a civilised society. The agricultural ground was described as abundantly fertile, where grain would grow in a plentiful harvest, and where ploughing would often turn up nuggets of gold, diamonds or pearls.

Major William John Richardson was appointed legate of Poyais, and MacGregor was able to persuade Richardson to allow him to take up residence in his country house, Oak Hall in Essex.

To back up his proposals, and give the whole scheme some credence, MacGregor opened a Poyaisian Legation to Britain in

London's Dowgate Hill and various land offices in Scotland. These
were located in Glasgow, Edinburgh and Stirling. Advertisements
appeared in Scottish newspapers such as that which appeared in
the *Stirling Journal* on Thursday 14 November 1822:

> Poyais
> (Price of Land only Three Shillings per Acre.)
> Notice is hereby given, that GRANTS of LAND in this Territory
> may still be obtained at the cheap rate of 3s per Acre; but that the
> price on the 15th inst. will be 4s per Acre; and that it will be
> advanced rapidly to a much higher rate.

The climate of Poyais is described as *mild* and *salubrious*, 'being
greatly superior to that of most other parts of the same vast
portion of the Globe.' Europeans generally retain their health and
activity to a good old age. 'To valetudinarians, and persons
advanced in life, it is the climate of Paradise.' An elegant historian
(Bryan Edwards) states, in *A Very Particular Memoir*, that 'every
variety of animal and vegetable nature for use of beauty, for food
or luxury, has been most liberally bestowed on this country', and
that 'with respect to food, the inhabitants seem almost exempted
from the curse entailed on our first parents.' Another writer states
it to be 'excelled by no country under the influence of British
dominion.' And 'the best poor man's country he ever saw or heard
of.' The advert went on to say:

> The soil is excellent, and every where well watered. – Horses,
> Black Cattle, Pigs, Poultry, &c., are numerous and can be purchased
> for stock at a very moderate price.
> The Lands are sold in square miles or sections of 640 acres each,
> or in subdivisions of 320, 160, 80, or 40 acres. Grants may be
> secured at the present price, by paying a deposit of 25 per cent and
> the remainder within six months thereafter, or, on application, a
> grant to the extent of the deposit will be given. Moreover, a

purchaser, or his agent, may select his land on presenting his title deed at the proper Office in the town of St Joseph's, in Poyais; but no Lands can for the present be purchased at any of the Offices in that country.

The original Grant is registered in the books of Council and Session, and in the Court of Chancery. Every other information as to the security of purchasers or otherwise, may be obtained by applying to the Land Offices in Edinburgh, Glasgow, or London.

Wm. Ker Thomson, Agent.

Poyais Land Office, 26, Nelson Street, Glasgow.

1st November 1822.

A first class Ship will sail from Leith Roads direct for Poyais, on or about the 1st of next month.

The first two ships did not leave Britain until the winter of 1822–3. The *Honduras Packet* left London on 10 September 1822 with 70 emigrants and the *Kennersley Castle* left the port of Leith on 22 January with around 200 emigrants on board, each of whom had signed up to settle in this wonderful country. Amongst them was a Mr Mauger, who had been employed in a bank in London, who was expecting to become the chief banker of the Bank of Poyais. MacGregor's sweet-talking also had a cobbler excited at the prospect of being the 'Official Shoemaker' to the Princess of Poyais. All the emigrants had their British currency converted into Poyaisian dollars, notes that MacGregor had printed in Scotland to further the scam.

The ships arrived at the bay off St Joseph's in March 1823. The sailors were excited at the prospect of arriving at the wonderful city they had heard of, but were unable to find it, or any port at which to land. Those who went ashore on small boats were informed by the natives that they had never heard of St Joseph's. They returned to their vessels, thinking they had landed at the wrong place.

Further investigation revealed that, yes, this was St Joseph's, and that it was little more than four or five run-down shacks, all that remained of a British colony of the eighteenth century.

The emigrants landed and discovered that the whole country and its amazing wealth was nothing but a sham, a massive con trick performed by MacGregor, who was back in Britain living a luxurious life thanks to the thousands of pounds he had tricked people out of.

Lieutenant Colonel Hector Hall, who had expected to become Governor of Poyais, tried to locate the *Honduras Packet,* which had been forced away from the shore by a storm. He left the settlers at St Joseph's busily trying to erect some form of shelter for themselves, to try to find a means of getting back to Britain.

The settlers at St Joseph's were unsure what to do. Some were stubbornly refusing to take part in the erection of shelters. Others were soon to suffer from various tropical diseases that struck at the British constitution. One settler is known to have committed suicide as soon as he realised that he had been swindled of his life's savings and was now stuck on the other side of the world without a penny to his name.

A rescue of the emigrants was arranged; the Chief Magistrate of the British colony of Belize, or British Honduras, sent ships to rescue them. The *Mexican Eagle* arrived in April 1823 and was able to take 60 settlers to Belize. Hector Hall also managed to return, accompanied by King George Frederic Augustus, who by this time had annulled the grant of land to MacGregor.

Further vessels were sent to Poyais to rescue the settlers, and they were taken back to Belize. Those who did not wish to settle there were given the opportunity to return to Britain on board the *Ocean,* which set sail on 1 August 1823, bound for London. The journey took 72 days. However, of the 240 emigrants who had left Leith, only 50 or so were able to make it back to Britain. In total it is reckoned that 180 died as a result of MacGregor's hoax.

A further five ships filled with emigrants had left Britain in the meantime, and when the fraud was discovered Royal Navy vessels were sent in hot pursuit to catch them and advise them to return home.

Back in Britain, when MacGregor was challenged about the kingdom he was promoting, and how it did not have any of the wonderful things he promised, he blamed the Belize settlers for robbing the Poyaisian settlers. The newspapers had a field day, and MacGregor was blamed for his audacity in the whole fraud.

Not all of the would-be settlers were critical of MacGregor. In Edinburgh a book was privately published in 1823. James Hastie, who had been one of the settlers who had made the journey to Poyais and managed to return, though without his two daughters, who had died of some tropical disease, wrote his account of the tale. In his *Narrative of a Voyage in the Ship* Kennersley Castle *from Leith Roads to Poyais*, he is not overtly critical of MacGregor; indeed he defends him, claiming that he was in no way to blame 'for the misfortunes which befell us'.

However, in November 1823 Gregor MacGregor had to make his escape from the pursuing creditors. He and his wife, and the two children they had at that time, crossed the English Channel and landed at Boulogne. They then moved to Paris, where they lived for some time, their third child being born there.

Although he realised that the authorities had nearly caught up with him, MacGregor still had not learned his lesson. He commenced his whole fraudulent scheme again, this time in Paris. However, on this occasion, he did not assert his sovereignty over Poyais, claiming instead that it was a republic, and that he was its Head of State. On 18 August 1825 he issued certificates for land in Poyais and again managed to con many hopeful settlers.

French passport officials began to question some of the people who had signed up to emigrate to Poyais, a country that the officials knew did not exist. Prior to the ships leaving port, they seized the vessel. An ex-army acquaintance of MacGregor's, Gustavus Butler Hippisley, had been appointed as his representative, and the French authorities arrested him. Others followed, and two months later MacGregor himself was arrested. On 6 April 1826 four Poyaisian promoters, MacGregor, Hippisley, Thomas Irving (MacGregor's secretary) and a Monsieur Lehuby, a business associate, were tried at court and charged with fraud.

The court decided that MacGregor, Hippisley and Irving could be released, as long as they were deported. Lehuby, who had escaped to Belgium and was being tried in his absence, was given most of the blame. However, the Belgian authorities then agreed to extradite him, and the trial started again on 10 July. Lasting four days, the trial acquitted MacGregor and the charges against Hippisley and Irving were withdrawn. Lehuby was found guilty of making false promises and was sentenced to thirteen months.

MacGregor decided to move back to Britain and opened up a Poyais land office in London's Threadneedle Street. He tried to sell new bonds investing in the country, but his reputation was in tatters and few were sold. 'Poyaisian New Three per cent Consolidated Stock' was issued with him titled 'President', rather than Cazique, in 1831. For a time he moved back to Scotland, living in Edinburgh from 1834, where he still tried to sell plots of land in Poyais. The last known case of him trying to sell land certificates took place in 1837. In Scotland in May 1838 his wife, 'Princess' Josefa, died.

The loss of his wife left MacGregor a broken man. He remained in Scotland for a few months, but the cheated investors were on his tail. He decided to emigrate to Venezuela – for at least in that country he was regarded as a hero and in the capital city, Caracas, there still stands a large monument in his honour. MacGregor was awarded a military pension in addition to back pay for the time he had been abroad, which allowed him to live in relative comfort for the remainder of his life. In Venezuela he commenced writing his autobiography, some of the handwritten notes for which are preserved in the National Archives of Scotland. MacGregor died in Caracas on 4 December 1845 and was buried with full military honours in the cathedral.

# 8

# *'A Great Farce of Pretended Devotion':*
# *The Buchanites*

The funeral party made its way from the house in Crocketford to the graveyard immediately behind it. It was the funeral of Andrew Innes, who had died in the middle of January 1846, an old and weak man. He had been declining since before Christmas, and had fallen and hurt himself. He died at 7 a.m., in his armchair, seemingly without pain. He had the distinction of being the last of the Buchanites.

A few weeks prior to his death, Innes had called three of his close friends and given them precise instructions on how he wished to be buried. He also confessed to them that he had the coffin and body of Elspeth Buchan in his possession, and that he wanted her buried underneath him, so that she could not rise again without wakening him. Accordingly, the grave was dug and the remains of Buchan were lowered into the ground. On top of her coffin Innes was laid, and not a 'sigh was heard, nor a tear shed' over him.

The Buchanites took their name from their leader, a woman named Elspeth Buchan. She was born in Banffshire in 1738 as Elspeth Simpson, daughter of John Simpson. It is thought that she was left an orphan by the age of three years, and that her parents

71

were keepers of a roadside ale-house, at Rothmackenzie, or Fetney-Can, which lies to the west of Banff, on the road to Portsoy. Elspeth received no schooling of any note and she lacked any religious guidance. She was brought up by strangers, who gave her little material or mental support, instead pushing her out to work herding cattle as soon as she was able.

Later descriptions of Elspeth claim that she was a very tall woman, and had considerable strength for a member of the female sex. She was given the nickname 'Luckie' Buchan, the term 'luckie' or 'lucky' being a Scots word for a female innkeeper.

It is reckoned that Elspeth's visions and wild thoughts began when she was alone in the fields. She later claimed that her first vision took place there when she was six or seven years of age. A cousin of Elspeth's, from whom she was given her name, discovered her plight whilst Elspeth was a teenager, and took her into her household. Elspeth was taught to read and write, and was given lessons in sewing and cooking. She was also introduced to the Episcopal form of worship.

Elspeth's cousin was to marry a wealthy West Indian tea planter, and they decided to emigrate to Jamaica. Elspeth was asked to join them, and she also went. Elspeth Buchan made her way to Greenock, where it was planned that she would board a vessel due to sail in a few days' time. However, she became distracted by the many goings-on in the port, and decided to abandon the thought of a life under the strict control of her cousin in Jamaica, and stay in Scotland instead.

Elspeth made her way to Glasgow in the 1750s, where she met with a Mrs Martin, wife of one of the partners of the Delftfield Pottery. This was an historic and famous pottery in Glasgow, located at that time at the Broomielaw. The Martins took pity on Elspeth, and decided to employ her as a maid in their home. She was by this time around 20 years of age.

Elspeth met a potter in the factory named Robert Buchan, and they fell in love. There is no confirmation that they ever married, but they certainly lived together as man and wife and she bore him numerous children, a number of whom were to die in infancy.

At some point, whether having been persuaded by his wife or not, Robert Buchan decided to move to Banffshire and there set up a pottery of his own. He, his wife, and their three surviving children (two daughters and one son), packed up and moved to Banffshire and established a business. The venture failed, and Robert Buchan returned to Glasgow, leaving his family behind. To earn money to keep them, Elspeth opened up a school for girls. This was reasonably successful to start with, for she had a number of pupils in her care. However, as time went by, she began to teach the Bible more and more, giving her interpretations of its meaning, as opposed to the more orthodox teachings of the time. Her views became so warped that soon the parents refused to send their children to her, and the school was boycotted. With no income, Elspeth left Banffshire and moved back to Glasgow in March 1781 with her three children.

Robert Buchan had become a member of the Burgh Secession Church and Elspeth Buchan joined it too when she arrived back in Glasgow. She became ever more deeply involved in religious dogma, and wrote extensively to ministers all over Scotland, but in particular to those in Aberdeenshire and Banffshire. One minister she corresponded with for a number of months was the Rev. Hugh White, minister of the Relief Church in Irvine, Ayrshire.

White had been brought up at St Ninians in Stirlingshire and had been licensed by the Church of Scotland, but failing to get a charge emigrated to America. There he became a professor of logic, and his beliefs became more extreme. He had become associated with the Shaker sect, which advocated free love. He was forced to leave his college and decided to return to Scotland. He joined the Relief Church and was ordained as a minister in Irvine on 3 July 1782. There he was noted as 'a coarse hewer', someone whose sermons were poorly crafted and roughly presented, and rather childish in his search for novelty value.

Writing in *The Scottish Gallovidian Encyclopedia* in 1824, John Mactaggart (1791–1830), who often wrote with his tongue in his cheek, described White as:

> A colleged priest, as he was termed – a fellow who had been bred up for the church in some university, but having a weak brain, unfit to hold the learning that was poured into it, he so became a fit subject for waiting upon Mrs Buchan, and frantic as she could possibly be. White, however, aided her cause very considerably. He was quite an Abbob Bekar to Mahomet. When the innocent country people heard that a real priest, a minister of the word, had become a Buchanite, they gathered in from all quarters, and became so likewise.

On one occasion in the spring of 1783, White was asked to assist in a communion service somewhere near Glasgow. In the congregation was Elspeth Buchan and White's sermon impressed her. She wrote to him once more, flattering him considerably, which he was pleased to accept, and more letters passed between them.

As time passed, Elspeth Buchan's assertions became ever more fanciful. Her main claim was that she had been born to be the saviour of the world. She claimed that she was the woman referred to in the Book of Revelation, Chapter 12, verses 1 and 5: 'there appeared a great wonder in heaven; a woman clothed with the sun, and the moon under her feet, and upon her head a crown of twelve stars. And she brought forth a man child, who was to rule all nations with a rod of iron: and her child was caught up unto God, and to his throne.' This woman was to come to earth to announce to the people that the second coming of Christ was due at any time. She also claimed that all who believed in her would pass into heaven without having to die, leaving behind all the unbelievers to their fate, living in conditions like Sodom and Gomorrah. She claimed that Rev. White was her spiritual 'man child.'

Whilst these claims may seem fanciful and nonsensical to the reader, both Buchan and White came to believe in them. In the first part of the summer of 1783 White invited Buchan to visit him at his manse in Irvine's Seagate. The house no longer exists, but stood around 50 yards to the south of Seagate Castle, on the west side of the street. Elspeth jumped at the chance to meet with him, and spent the next three weeks in his home. Whilst in the town she preached and soon gained a following from those who found her explanations of difficult passages from the Bible helpful.

Elspeth Buchan believed in a variety of things, such as companionate marriage which did not recognise official wedding ceremonies. She also followed the socialist view of private property. White agreed with these doctrines, and his acceptance of them shocked many of those in his church. When Elspeth returned to Glasgow after her three-week stay, White was visited by a deputation of elders and other members of the church and was asked to renounce his heterodox opinions – but he refused to do so. The elders took matters further, reporting him to the Presbytery of Glasgow. An inquiry took place, after which the Presbytery ejected him from his charge. He had been a minister in the church for only 17 months.

Rev. White commenced independent services at his home in the Seagate once he had been thrown out of his church. Within a short time Elspeth Buchan moved from Glasgow to join him and they formed a preaching society. Elspeth was given the rather grand title of 'Friend Mother in the Lord'. The congregation outgrew the Seagate house and soon services were being held in a tent in the back garden. The sound of the sect's singing and praising attracted a lot of attention, and this, as well as the blasphemous names they created for themselves, disturbed the locals. Often, when services were underway, people threw dirt and stones over the wall onto the tent, forcing the service to be abandoned.

The sect moved from Rev. White's garden to a new building in the town's Glasgow Vennel, which still stands today on the west side of the street. This was the property of Patrick Hunter, a writer, who had become a follower of Buchan and her beliefs, previously being an elder in the Relief Church. Hunter had been of some standing in the town for many years, being burgh fiscal and occasionally acting as depute town clerk. He was a prominent businessman, operating shipping and coal merchants. Hunter's house in the Glasgow Vennel was bounded to one side by the home of Provost Charles Hamilton. He was a small and thin man, with a crooked back, earning him the unfortunate soubriquet of 'Humpy Hunter'.

The services held in the Vennel were still subject to attacks from the locals, who found the Buchanites' beliefs alien to their own. The homes of those who belonged to the sect were subject to abuse, and were often attacked, with windows being broken and missiles thrown at them. On one occasion Hunter's home was the target of the mob, and they broke all of his windows and smashed down his door. Elspeth Buchan was inside and she tried to make her escape by a back route. However, the mob caught her and she was dragged through the streets of Irvine. Her clothes were ripped and objects were thrown at her. Elspeth was dragged as far as Stewarton, on the road to Glasgow, before she managed to escape.

Buchan made her way back to Irvine, keeping to the fields, away from the public roads. By the time she arrived back in the town she was almost naked, and her body was covered in blood from the wounds and cuts she had received. It was still early in the morning and she was able to reach Rev. White's house without being noticed. Mrs Magdalen Gibson was in the manse and she dressed Elspeth's wounds, cleaned her up, and put her to bed.

Word of Buchan's return to Irvine leaked out, and a riot broke out in the town. The mob made its way to the Seagate and gathered outside White's manse. Feelings were high, and there was a danger that someone was going to be injured. The town council convened in haste, and sent orders to Patrick Hunter that he was to arrange for Elspeth Buchan to be forcibly removed from the town. He found a horse and cart and placed her on it with Mrs Gibson, who was to look after Buchan. As the horse and cart made its way through the town the locals gazed from the sides of the road. Many shouted and hurled abuse at the party, and many of the burgh residents walked behind the cart, bawling and shouting as they went.

Elspeth Buchan was returned to her husband in Glasgow, and after making a recovery decided to return to Irvine once more. She continued preaching, trying to convert others to her sect. This time the burgesses and officials of the town decided that they would pursue an order banning her from the town. They contacted the magistrates of the burgh, who were Lord Provost Archibald Montgomerie, 11th Earl of Eglinton (1726–96), Bailie James Shaw and Bailie Hugh Watt, and persuaded them to act to expel Buchan. At 10 a.m. on 4 May 1784, the day of the May Fair, or 'Cow Fair' as it was known locally, the magistrates met and decided unanimously that Elspeth Buchan should be expelled from the burgh two hours hence.

The streets of Irvine were filled with people from the burgh and surrounding areas, all there to enjoy themselves and meet others on the day of the fair. The bailies and constables of the town made their way to the Seagate, where Buchan was lodged with the Whites. When they opened the door to make their way into the street they found that it was filled to capacity, and they had to force their way through the heaving crowds.

Although it was only Elspeth Buchan who was obliged to leave Irvine, 45 of her followers made up their minds to join her. These people were mainly female, but there were one or two men in the company. So convinced were they by Buchan's teachings that they reckoned that this was the second coming of Christ. Her followers walked out of their homes, leaving the doors open wide, their belongings within and their cattle tied to the poles in their gardens.

The entourage made its way up the Seagate to the High Street, then down through Irvine Cross to the Townhead. All the way the massive crowds hurled abuse at the sect, throwing objects and trying to push Buchan to the ground. The magistrates tried to protect Buchan as much as they could, but found it difficult to keep the thousands of folk back from her. Around one mile out of the burgh the magistrates left the sect to their own devices. One drunken sailor ran at Buchan and removed her cap, grabbing at her hair and yanking a handful from her head. He yelled to the crowd, 'I have got a right good handful of her hair!' The authorities turned a blind eye to his actions.

A young John Galt (1779–1839), later to become one of Scotland's greatest novelists, witnessed the expulsion. He noted that they shouted that they were on the way to the New Jerusalem. In fact, the young Galt became so embroiled that he joined the entourage. It was only when his mother grabbed him by the ear and pulled him back under her command, that he came to his senses and didn't follow further.

Once they were free from the braying crowd, the Buchanites gathered together and began marching along the Kilmarnock road. As they made their way they sang psalms and yelled loud Hallelujahs!

The Buchanites marched to Kilmaurs, where they spent the night. On the following day they were joined by Rev. White and others, before they headed south through Mauchline and Cumnock to Nithsdale. They followed the road down the valley through Sanquhar and Thornhill, before stopping at New Cample Farm, which lies by the side of the Cample Water, one mile to the south of Thornhill, on the Dumfries road. Here they found lodgings in an old barn, the tenant, Thomas Davidson, being sympathetic to their needs.

The sect began to work, building a commune for themselves. A large barn-like building was raised, covered over with a thatched roof. Within the loft of the building they formed one large dormitory, in which all members of the sect slept together on piles of heather. This building became known as Buchan Ha', or hall.

Here the sect set their philosophy in stone. Their main belief was that the coming of Christ, or the millennium as they termed it, was soon at hand, and that if they believed then they would be taken into the air, transformed into His likeness, and would live with Him for 1,000 years. They believed that no sin existed within the believers, and that it was futile to pray for the pardon of sins. It was believed that the soul could not leave the body. They believed that goods should be owned communally, that marriage was pointless – instead there should be a community of women, and that Elspeth was the Third Person in the Godhead and that she would lead them to a second coming.

The members were quite a mixed bunch. Elspeth Buchan's two adult daughters were members, but she later was to claim, as part of her belief that she was a daughter of God, that these earthly daughters were not really hers. John Gibson was appointed as treasurer, and Janet Grant, who had been Mrs Muir, was given the task of looking after the clothing as she had had a clothes shop in Irvine.

The Buchanites were known to Robert Burns, who wrote about them in a letter to his cousin, James Burness, on 3 August 1784:

We have been surprised with one of the most extraordinary Phenomena in the moral world, which, I dare say, has happened in the course of this last Century. – We have had a party of the Presbytery Relief as they call themselves, for some time in this country. A pretty thriving society of them has been in the Burgh of Irvine for some years past, till about two years ago, a Mrs Buchan from Glasgow came among them, & in a short time made many converts among them & among others their Preacher, one Mr Whyte, who upon that account has continued however, to preach in private to this party, & was supported, both he, & their spiritual Mother as they affect to call old Buchan, by the contributions of the rest, several of whom were in good circumstances; till in spring last the Populace rose & mobbed the old leader Buchan, & put her out of the town . . . Their tenets are a strange jumble of enthusiastic jargon, among others, she pretends to give them the Holy Ghost by breathing on them, which she does with postures & practices that are scandalously indecent; they have likewise disposed of all their effects & hold a community of goods, & live nearly an idle life, carrying on a great farce of pretended devotion in barns, & woods, where they lodge and lye all together, & hold likewise a community of women, as it is another of their tenets that they can commit no moral sin. – I am personally acquainted with most of them, & I can assure you the above mentioned are facts.

Support for the Buchanites grew to some extent, and it is recorded in the *New Statistical Account* of Ayrshire that Rev. Francis Kelly of Northampton was a supporter, in May 1784 'confessing [Buchan] in the fullest manner to be of God'. Others joined them at New Cample, including Lieutenant Charles E. Conyers, who relinquished his post in the marines. A few from the English side of the border felt they would like to join, but their membership remained around fifty.

Each time a new convert was introduced, much was made of it, and they spread the word. Many people from all over Scotland corresponded with them, as well as a few ministers of the Church of England who wrote letters on a regular basis out of curiosity.

The Buchanites, in promoting themselves, published much of this correspondence, and in 1785 decided to publish a book on their beliefs. Entitled *The Divine Dictionary, or, a Treatise indicted by Holy Inspiration*, this volume only extended to two parts before it was stopped. Those who read it denounced it as blasphemous, which was very injurious to their cause. Within the book was the notice:

The truths contained in this publication, the writer received from the Spirit of God in that woman, predicted in Rev. xii. 1. though they are not written in the same simplicity as delivered – by a babe in the love of God, HUGH WHITE. Revised and approven of by ELSPAT SIMPSON.

Elspeth Buchan often tried to predict things, one of her most dangerous predictions, or most stupid, was of the day she and any believers would be called to heaven, without dying. Accordingly, around July 1784 Elspeth Buchan declared that the day for her to be called to the heavens had arrived. She climbed the low hill opposite New Cample called Templand Mount. A number of her followers went with her and built platforms on which they were to lie, awaiting a gust of heavenly wind to draw them to the regions above. Buchan's platform was positioned higher than the others and she attempted to perform a miracle in which she was transfigured and ascended to heaven.

The Buchanites took up their positions on the platforms, lying facing the heavens. Prior to this they had cut all their hair apart from a single tuft on the uppermost part of the scalp, which was left so that the angels would have something to grab to pull them upward. They all lay awaiting the call, and things seemed promising when the wind rose, blowing over and around them. However, the wind became so strong that it blew over Elspeth's platform causing her to fall to the ground and out of her trance. The failure of the miracle caused many of her followers to question much of what she said, but most still clung to the sect and remained part of it.

Another of Luckie Buchan's schemes was that the group should fast for 40 days. It was reckoned that by losing weight the group would be much lighter and therefore more readily able to ascend heavenward. The sect was keen to start with, avoiding food and drink. However after a few days a number of them became ill, for lack of fluid, whereupon Elspeth relented, allowing drinks.

However, starvation became too much for most, and within a few days more they began to eat. Elspeth again claimed that the failure of this experiment was due to the lack of faith of the participants.

A visitor to the commune in 1784 reported that they seemed to be quite decent folk, and that he 'found them a very temperate, civil, discreet, and sensible people, very free in declaring their principles, when they were attended to; but most of their visitants behaved in a rude, wicked, and abandoned way'.

These visitants persecuted the Buchanites at New Cample. The kirk sessions of Penpont and Closeburn tried to have them charged with profligacy or blasphemy, but these attempts failed. Many locals began to believe that she practised witchcraft and on 24 December 1784 a mob attacked Buchan Ha'. The authorities in Dumfriesshire took the side of the Buchanites, and 42 of the rioters were tried by the sheriff on a charge of breach of the peace. However, the Buchanites refused to prosecute those who had rioted against them, and most refused to confirm any injuries they received during the rabble. When the first Buchanite was placed in prison for suppressing the truth they were forced to testify.

In time the Dumfriesshire authorities decided that they would need to expel the Buchanites, and so an order was issued demanding that they leave the county by 10 March 1787.

The Buchanites decided that they could only be safe if they had a stretch of ground of their own. Accordingly, they moved on, and made their way down through Nithsdale before crossing into Galloway. At first they spent some time at Tarbreoch, in the parish of Kirkpatrick Durham, where they were given the use of an old house by a sympathetic gentleman. They continued to hold open-air meetings, and these attracted many inquisitive locals, some of whom joined in their praises. However, within a short time the novelty wore off and they were left alone. It is reckoned that the Buchanites made no converts after they moved from Buchan Ha'.

Three months later the Buchanite sect was able to take on the lease of Auchengibbert farm at Crocketford, nine miles west of Dumfries. It occupies the land between the Milton and Auchenreoch lochs. Rev. White was named as the leaseholder, which was to become significant later. They paid a rental of one shilling per acre.

The members of the sect laboured on local farms, and on one occasion worked in the fields of Rev. Dr James Muirhead, minister of Urr. During September 1787 they were gathering in the harvest of corn on his fields along with others, who had noticed nothing untoward of their fellow labourers, when a woman in her fifties came towards them, none other than Elspeth Buchan herself. Immediately the Buchanites became agitated and excited, threw down their tools and began to embrace each other. They then walked slowly towards Luckie Buchan and made a circle round her. Raising their hands in the air they began singing one of the sect's own hymns:

Let no one imagine we here mean to tarry,
    Although to the parish of Urr we have come;
By us Auchengibbert has only been taken
    To rest in, as onward we march to our home.

The commune used their various skills to build up their reputation as good workers. A local worthy noted that 'their heids may be a wee bit aff, but they're gran' wi' their hauns'. The group worked the fields with considerable success. They had a joiner capable of making timber objects, and they built barns and byres at Auchengibbert. Some of the women spun wool, and their woollen goods were in demand throughout the south-west. Linen produced by them was in demand by the gentry of the county.

Elspeth Buchan proposed yet another miracle in which she and the believers would be called to heaven. Arranged in a similar fashion as the Borland Mount incident, they lay on platforms on the low hill at Auchengibbert. Having lain there for much of the day, with nothing happening, they were forced to abandon the experiment.

Some of the Buchanites began to waver in their belief, and some made it known that they were planning to return to Irvine. Elspeth Buchan tried to prevent this, and it is recorded that she would sometimes lock up potential deserters and submerge them every day in freezing waters. Her fantasies and predictions became ever stranger in an effort to keep her followers.

One of the adherents who managed to escape the control of the sect in 1786 reported:

> The distribution of provisions she kept in her own hand, and took special care that they should not pamper their bodies with too much food, and every one behoved to be entirely directed by her. The society being once scarce of money, she told them she had a revelation, informing her they should have a supply of cash from heaven: accordingly, she took one of the members out with her, and caused him to hold two corners of a sheet, while she held the other two. Having continued for a considerable time without any shower of money falling upon it, the man at last tired, and left Mrs Buchan to hold the sheet herself. Mrs Buchan, in a short time after, came in with £5, and upbraided the man for his unbelief, which she said was the only cause that prevented it from coming sooner. Many of the members, however, easily accounted for this pretended miracle, and shrewdly suspected that the money came from her own hoard. That she had a considerable purse was not to be doubted, for she fell on many ways to rob the members of everything they had of value.

A number of Buchanites returned to Irvine. Patrick Hunter and his children were brought back to the town under a *meditatione fugae* warrant. This type of warrant was usually issued by a creditor to apprehend a debtor on the pretext that the debtor was expected to abscond without paying his debts. It is thought that the warrant was brought by his wife, Frances Hunter, who was a member of the Stane Castle family. The debt may have been money due to her for her keep. Hunter was thus brought back to Irvine where his family subsequently kept him apart from any contact with any member of the sect. Even letters sent by members of the sect in Galloway were prevented from reaching him.

Despite being shielded from contact with the Buchanites, Hunter apparently still seemed to believe that Elspeth Buchan was immortal. When he was told of her death in 1791, by a horse-dealer who had been at Dumfries market, he responded, 'Oh, No! That is not the case, and never will be in this world.' The dealer, in his humorous way, replied, 'Well, if she is not dead, her friends have played her a devilish trick, for they have buried her.'

Mrs Hunter had herself been connected with the Buchanites, but joined the Established Church in Irvine. According to the kirk session minute of 18 November 1787 she appeared before the session. There she 'professed her sorrow on account of being misled by the errors of Mrs Buchan and desired to be restored to Christian privilege – the session agreed to restore her accordingly.'

A *meditatione fugae* warrant was raised at Kirkcudbright sheriff court by John Gibson, who had been a master builder in Irvine. He had joined the sect and had advanced them £85, but this was not repaid. Buchan and White were arrested, and taken to Kirkcudbright where they were imprisoned. A Buchanite sympathiser, Thomas Bradley from Hartlepool, paid the bail money to have them released. However, White put in a counter-claim against Bradley for board and lodgings, so that he lost out considerably in his association with the sect.

Elspeth Buchan took ill, and at length died on 29 March 1791. Prior to her death she called the members of the sect round, and explained to them what would happen to her. She claimed that once she appeared to die her spirit would return to her body at some point and bring it back to life. When this would take place depended on their devoutness. If they did not believe her, then they would have to wait ten years before the spirit returned, and if they were unprepared then it would be 50 years before her spirit came back to lead them to the New Jerusalem.

Immediately after her death, her corpse was secretly taken to the kirkyard of Kirkgunzeon and buried. However, after a few days the sect began to think of Buchan's need of her body, so at night they went back to Kirkgunzeon and disinterred the body. It was brought back to Auchengibbert and kept under the kitchen hearthstone.

With Buchan gone, Rev. White became the only leader, and it is recorded that he ruled his followers with a rod of iron. He sold the stock reared on the farm, and the money was paid to himself. White decided that he would emigrate to America, and he persuaded 30 others to join him there. Only around 12–14 of Buchan's more fanatical members remained in Scotland.

With the Rev. White having relinquished the lease of Auchengibbert, the faithful remnant had to find a new place to stay. They took on the lease of Larghill, a hill farm on the other side of Crocketford from Auchengibbert. They remained there until 1808.

The Buchanites remained an industrious lot, respected by their neighbours. They were kindly and mannerly, and their carts which they used to transport goods to market, were inscribed 'Mercy's Property'. In later years this was changed to 'The people of Larghill'.

With a growing fund, the commune was able to purchase around five acres of ground at Crocketford, or the Nine Mile Bar, in 1800. Some of the members moved here, building cottages which were to become the start of a new village. The first house that they built was named Newhouse, and it was ready in 1802. In a plot of ground behind this they established a small cemetery, so that they could all be buried in the same place, awaiting the return of Elspeth Buchan to collect them.

All this time the corpse of Buchan had been kept by her adherents, and it was many days before they decided to straighten it out or dress it, always expecting her to return and bring it back to life. However, as days passed the smell became so horrid that they were obliged to take it to the barn where it was laid in an open coffin. Word of the corpse being stored thus leaked to the neighbours, who were so shocked at the thought that they applied to the local justice of the peace to issue an order that Buchan should be buried. The sect eventually agreed, and she was supposedly buried in the cemetery at Newhouse.

In 1808 the last members of the sect moved from Larghill into Crocketford. The last survivor of the sect was Andrew Innes, who died in January 1846. He had been a young lad when he joined the sect, and kept to its beliefs long after most of the rest had either died or given up.

In the closing years the Buchanites were seen as being wild fanatics. In Mactaggart's *Gallovidian Encyclopedia*, written in 1824, he noted that they were still living at Crocketford, and that Elspeth Buchan . . .

. . . would allow none of her followers to marry, or have any love-dealings with other; so the tribe soon weeded away and became thin. It is said that there were many bastard bairnies appeared amongst them; but that they hardly ever let them behold the light. Be this as it may, their general character all along has been quite harmless. They were, and yet are, a very industrious people, and have been long unmatched at making Wee Wheels and Chackreels, plying the turning-loom to great perfection. They are all, however, of rather a wild frantic nature, and seem to want 'some pence of the shilling, a penny or more.'

# 9

# *The Forgers: Arthur Smith, John Graham and James Steele*

The forging of cash has been undertaken in Scotland for centuries. Today it is a comparatively simple task to use a scanner and a laser printer to produce fairly accurate copies of banknotes, which many unscrupulous individuals have passed over in shops or bars. Fake coins, in particular pound coins, regularly turn up in your change, the average customer not taking the time to check if the handful of coins they have been given is genuine.

In the seventeenth century Arthur Smith lived in the Caithness area. He was a notorious forger of coins, and was employed by the 'Wicked' Earl of Caithness, George Sinclair (1565–1643), a man notorious for his feuds with neighbouring clans, who was responsible for various battles and murders between them. So impoverished had Sinclair become that he tracked down Arthur Smith and employed him to forge coins of the realm so that he could pay his debts and live as he was accustomed.

Smith had previously been arrested for forging coins and following a trial he was condemned to death. However, Lord Elphinstone, who was the Lord Treasurer of Scotland at the time, felt that this sentence was too harsh and on his intervention Smith was given a pardon.

**Above.** Dunfallandy House, near Pitlochry, Perthshire, which 'Lord Battenberg' leased for some time, running up thousands of pounds' worth of debt (Dane Love)

**Left.** Nelson's Column, London, which Arthur Furguson is said to have sold to an unsuspecting American for £6,000 in 1923 (Author's Collection)

**Above.** Gordon Hotel, Tomintoul, restored by Anthony Williams, the 'Laird of Tomintoul', using money taken from a secret account held by the Metropolitan Police in London for eliciting information that could lead to the arrest of major criminals (Dane Love)

**Below.** The Clockhouse Restaurant, Tomintoul, another of Anthony Williams' projects using stolen money (Dane Love)

**Above.** Frank Searle, the self-styled Loch Ness monster expert, at his Loch Ness Information Centre (Ken MacPherson)

**Below.** Burns Temple cartoon on a postcard issued at the time by Mrs Tommy Rodger, Kilmarnock (Author's Collection)

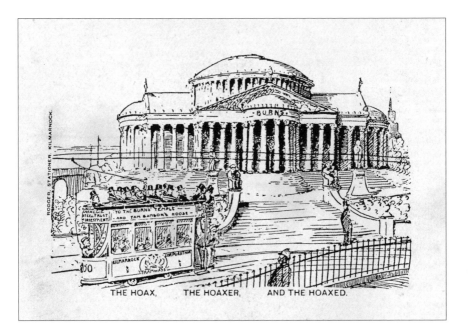

THE HOAX,       THE HOAXER,       AND THE HOAXED.

The fake war-hero, 'Sir' Alan McIlwraith, and his fiancée ready to attend a charity ball and no doubt talk of his list of brave achievements (Ian MacNicol)

**left.** 'Sir' Gregor MacGregor, the self-styled 'Prince of Poyais', an unscrupulous man who enticed whole families to travel to the other side of the world to set up home in a non-existent country over which he claimed to have territorial rights (National Museums Scotland, Licensor: www.scran.ac.uk)

**Below.** Inverardran House, which stands to the east of Crianlarich in Perthshire, the birthplace of Gregor MacGregor (Dane Love)

# PROCLAMATION,

## *To the Inhabitants of the Territory of Poyais.*

POYERS!

On the 29th April 1820, the King of the Mosquito Nation, by a deed, executed at Cape Gracias a Dios, granted to me and my heirs for ever, the Territory of Poyais.

The moment that the situation of affairs in Colombia would permit me, I have hastened to assure you of my firm and unalterable determination to come and spend the remainder of my days, I trust, in peace and tranquillity, amongst you.

POYERS! It shall be my constant study to render you happy, and to exert myself in improving your situation, by every means in my power.

The Territory of Poyais shall be an asylum only for the industrious and honest,—none others shall be admitted amongst us; and THOSE, I trust, you will receive with open arms, as brothers and fellow-citizens.

With a view of avoiding a misunderstanding with our Spanish neighbours, which, under *all circumstances*, would be disadvantageous to both parties, I have this day published a MANIFESTO, addressed to the AUTHORITIES and INHABITANTS of the adjoining SPANISH AMERICAN PROVINCES of HONDURAS and NICARAGUA, giving them the most positive assurances, " that I have no other views *here*, than those which my duty as Chief of this Territory inspires."

Animated with the hope of establishing our neutrality upon a safe and solid basis, as well as to enable me to take the most active measures for procuring you religious and moral instructors, the implements of husbandry, and persons to guide and assist you in the cultivation of the valuable productions for which our soil and climate are so well adapted, I have determined upon visiting Europe; and in consequence, have this day appointed the Governor of San Andres, H. E. BRIGADIER GENERAL GEORGE WOODBINE, M. G. C. to act and take upon him the office of my VICE-CAZIQUE during my absence; charging him to pay the most paternal attention to your interests, and with positive orders to observe the most strict neutrality with respect to the adjoining provinces of HONDURAS and NICARAGUA, as the most certain and sure means of encouraging emigrants to come and settle in our country, and of avoiding the expense of maintaining a large military force, at a moment when all our resources are required for carrying into effect the establishments already projected, and in progress; and I confidently trust, that you will shew to the said Vice-Cazique that respect and attachment which the citizens of all countries are bound to pay and feel towards those who lawfully command, particularly when they exercise their authority with justice and impartiality.

POYERS! I now bid you farewell for a while, in the full confidence that the measures I have adopted for your security, defence, government, and future prosperity, will be fully realized; and I trust, that through the kindness of Almighty Providence, I shall be again enabled to return amongst you, and that then it will be my pleasing duty to hail you as affectionate friends, and yours to receive me as your faithful Cazique and Father.

*By H. H. Command,*
**G. DRUMMOND,**
*Secretary.*

*Given at Head Quarters, in the Camp of*
*Rio Seco, this 13th day of April 1821.*

**GREGOR,** Cazique of Poyais.

A TRUE COPY OF THE ORIGINAL.
THOMAS STRANGEWAYS, *Aid-de-camp,*
*and Captain 1st Native Poyer Regiment.*

**Above.** Proclamation to the inhabitants of the non-existent province of Poyais, 1821, issued by Gregor MacGregor (National Library of Scotland, Licensor: www.scran.ac.uk)

**Right.** The Buchanite Meeting House, located in the Glasgow Vennel, Irvine, where followers of 'Lucky' Buchan celebrated her strange Biblical beliefs (Dane Love)

**Above.** Newhouse, Crocketford, built by the Buchanites as their new home once they had been hounded out of various villages for their heretical beliefs. (Dane Love)

**Below left.** Frontispiece of Joseph Train's *History of the Buchanites*, showing one of the last Buchanites, Andrew Innes, sitting at his fireside (Author's Collection)

**Below right.** Frontispiece of *The Divine Dictionary*, compiled by Elspeth Buchan, 1785, in which she gives guidance to the followers of her weird sect (Author's Collection)

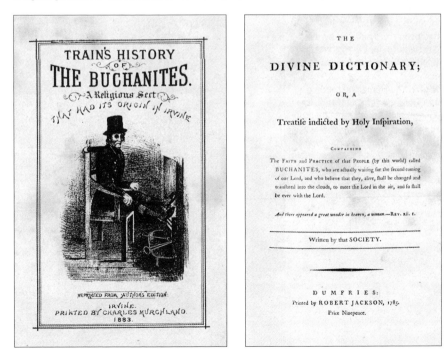

**Above.** Drumblair House, near Huntly in Aberdeenshire, which was leased by George Williams as a shooting lodge, prior to his arrest for leaving behind a trail of debt (Dane Love)

**Right.** A sketch of the arch-forger, 'Antique' Smith, as shown in a contemporary newspaper (Burns Monument Trust)

# THE MSS. FRAUDS.

*Evening Despatch.* — 3 Dec. 1892.

### PORTRAIT OF "ANTIQUE" SMITH.

This is a portrait of the man who will be known as "Antique" Smith, the forger of the MSS. It was sketched yesterday by one of our artists without the permission of Mr Smith.

**Above.** Forged letter by 'Antique' Smith claimed to be from Robert Burns to Rev John McMath (Burns Monument Trust)

**Below.** The great forger, 'Antique' Smith's signature. (Burns Monument Trust)

THE GENUINE SIGNATURE OF THE FORGER.

**Left.** Dr James Graham, the proprietor of the upmarket brothel, the Temple of Health, pursuing a Miss Dunbar in Edinburgh

**Below.** Ayr Low Green, where the fake minister, 'Rev' Thomas Clifford, preached and was able to build up sufficient followers in order to establish a church (Author's Collection)

**Left.** The poet, James MacPherson, who claimed to have discovered ancient Gaelic verses which he translated into English, causing a world-wide sensation (Author's Collection)

**Below.** Ossian's Stone, near Birnam, Perthshire, one of many places that was claimed to have had connections with the ancient Celtic hero promoted by James MacPherson (Dane Love)

**Above.** Ossian's Hall, near Birnam, Perthshire, now owned by the National Trust for Scotland, but which was a folly built in honour of the fables of Ossian (Dane Love)

**Below.** Balavil House, Kingussie, home of James 'Ossian' MacPherson, and built with the considerable earnings he made from his fake poetry (Dane Love)

**Left.** James MacPherson's Monument, Kingussie (Dane Love)

**Below.** Airlie Castle, Angus, which was leased for a time by Monty and Martha Spencer, prior to them moving out and taking many of the antiques with them (Dane Love)

**Right.** Airlie Castle, Angus, detail of gateway from MacGibbon & Ross (Author's Collection)

**Below.** Plan of Pelican Rapids, Minnesota, United States, in 1884, shortly after the great fraudster, Lord Gordon-Gordon proposed changing it into the city of Loomis, and which resulted in many residents being forced to sell up to pay debts that he had amassed (Author's Collection)

Smith went to Caithness where he set up his own unofficial mint. This was apparently located in a subterranean chamber under Castle Sinclair, which stands on a wave-battered sandstone headland, two miles to the north of Wick. The mint was located at a spot known as the Gote, and tradition claims that there was a secret passage linking the cavern with the earl's bedchamber. Only two people were allowed access to the mint, Smith himself and Lord Caithness. He remained employed by Sinclair, making hundreds of false coins, for between seven and eight years.

The coins produced by Smith went into local circulation, and soon they had spread all over Caithness, Sutherland, Ross-shire and into Orkney. During a visit to the area in 1611, Sir Robert Gordon, brother of the Earl of Sutherland, noticed the false coins and, on his return to England, he informed the king of the scale of the problem. In 1612 King James ordered the Privy Council to grant a commission to Donald Mackay of Farr (1591–1649), latterly 1st Lord Reay, Sir Robert Gordon and John Gordon, the younger of Embo, to capture Smith and bring him to Edinburgh for trial.

The Gordons and Mackay made their way to Thurso in 1613, where they were able to arrest Arthur Smith at his own home in the town. However, in the turmoil that ensued John Sinclair of Stirkoke, nephew of the wicked earl, was killed. Another of Caithness' relatives, James Sinclair, brother of the Laird of Dun, was severely wounded. The Gordons and Mackay decided to take matters into their own hands to ensure that Smith did not escape – they shot him.

The tumult at Thurso was reported to the Privy Council – by both sides. The Earl of Caithness, who had been in Edinburgh at the time, and his supporters complained that the Gordons and Mackay had killed one of his relatives, wounded another, and had taken the law into their own hands and killed Smith. The Gordons and Mackay complained to the council that Lord Berriedale, Caithness' son, and various other followers of Caithness had resisted the king's commission and had attacked those who were carrying it out.

The Privy Council met and for three days considered the evidence from both sides concerning the riot that had resulted in death and injury. Both parties were bound over to keep the peace and on 17 July 1612 the council granted a warrant for deserting the criminal prosecutions between the earls of Caithness and Sutherland. In December 1613 Donald Mackay and some others received a remission for their part in the death of Sinclair of Stirkoke.

In 1763 John Graham was appointed the grammar school teacher at Kilmarnock where he was noted for his 'brilliant talents and engaging manner'. He was a significant resident of the town, and was precentor in the church and custodian of the parish records. He had been born in Perthshire in 1734, the son of a farmer. He became efficient in Greek and Latin and studied at Glasgow University, one of his lecturers being Dr Adam Smith, of *Wealth of Nations* fame. Graham was training for the ministry, but on his father's death he had to give up studying due to a lack of money and thus did not complete his degree. He became tutor to the son of a landed gentleman in the south of Scotland, and when the pupil himself went to Glasgow University, Graham was able to return once more, passing his Master of Arts degree with distinction.

In 1779, after teaching in Kilmarnock for 16 years, he became acquainted with a man named Hunter, described in Graham's subsequent biography, *Genuine Memoirs of the Life of John Graham, AM*, as 'a miscreant fellow, an adventurer and sharper, who, under the pretence of being a man of fortune, cheated many industrious men of their all; and would have been punished as a cheat, had he not made his escape to London'. Hunter persuaded Graham to move to London, where he reckoned he should set up a new school. It took a week to sell all of Graham's furniture and books at auction. His household goods disposed of for a decent price, Graham and his wife and eight children plus a servant left for London. He opened a school at Pancras Wells but his reputation meant nothing in London, and he found it difficult to attract sufficient paying scholars to keep his large house and school.

As his cash ran out he was forced to sell much of his new furniture to pay outstanding debts. Eventually he had nothing left, and it was then he commenced forging banknotes. He met with an engraver and he discovered that he could afford to purchase a printing plate for ten pound notes. He paid for a plate and a few days later returned to collect it. However, the engraver decided to play it safe and informed the city magistrate that Graham had a counterfeit plate.

The police went to Graham's house and arrested him. He was tried at the capital's Old Bailey courthouse in October 1781. The judge told him that his life would be spared since he had not had the chance to print any notes, but that he would be sentenced to six months' imprisonment for proposing to commit fraud.

On his release, John Graham returned to forgery to try to pay off his debts. He didn't use the plate, as it had been taken by the police and destroyed. Instead he acquired a few Bank of England £15 notes and removed the 'een' with bleach. In their place he printed a 'y' using a block of type specially made for the purpose. Thus he was able to convert £15 notes into £50 notes.

To get rid of the new notes Mrs Graham was dressed up like a lady and travelled in style in a post-chaise to various shops and businesses – only someone of considerable standing could afford £50 notes so she had to look the part. For a time the Grahams got away with their scam, but eventually the forgeries were detected by a bank, and Graham was high on the police's list of suspects.

Policemen followed Mr and Mrs Graham to Southampton, where they were arrested at an inn by Mr Wright of Tothill Fields, Bridewell. He had apparently followed them from Winchester, where John Graham had met a Mr Tyrie, who was held in gaol there. Graham had given Tyrie half a guinea, which he was to use to buy implements that would allow him to break free. He did not manage this, and was soon executed at Portsmouth for high treason.

The Grahams were tried and blamed each other in court. The judge found both of them guilty and ordered that they should be hanged. Mrs Graham, however, had her sentence reduced. John Graham was taken to the gallows at Tyburn in London and executed on 15 October 1782.

A more recent case of forgery took place in Edinburgh in the 1920s. Robert Ramsay, a joiner, and James Steele, an electrician, both lived in a flat at 13 Caledonian Road, in the city's West End, just off Dalry Road. They also rented business premises at Murieston Crescent Lane, further along Dalry Road, next to the railway line, which to anyone who happened to be passing appeared to be a workshop for the repair and service of radios, or wirelesses as they were known at the time. The building was two storeys in height, built of brick, and was surrounded by lock-ups and other stores. Few people ever ventured down the lane, which meant that the forgers could work undisturbed at their task.

Both men were 45 years of age, and in their youth had been apprenticed in the same workshop as joiners. At the outbreak of the First World War both men served with distinction, Steele serving in France, where he was seriously wounded in the shoulder and lost the sight in his left eye. Ramsay spent the war on service in India. On their return they were both keen experimenters with electricity and electromagnetism, and were trying to raise a patent concerning electro-plating and electro-typing. However, this did not come to anything, and in 1927 they started counterfeiting coins.

At their trial the Solicitor General gave an account of how the coins were made, and stated that it was very similar to how legitimate coins were made at the Royal Mint. Steele and Ramsay bought nickel and at first made rough coins from it. They were then coated with a silver covering and stamped. After this the coin was blackened, to give the appearance of age.

It was not the quality of Ramsay and Steele's coins that led to their arrest; it was the method they had employed to get their coins into circulation. Apparently, on a regular basis, a young boy was sent on an errand to the sub post office, located in Elm Row, at Leith Walk, in order to buy postal orders. Each postal order he purchased was paid for by a 1920 half crown. However, the assistant, a Miss Tennent, gradually became aware of the regularity of these purchases, and there was one thing that caught her interest in the matter – each of the half crowns used in payment appeared to be brand new, despite being almost ten years old.

Miss Tennent took some of the coins to the local bank to ask if they could verify if they were genuine or not. The coins were passed around the tellers and the bank manager, and all declared that they were real. However, Miss Tennent was still not satisfied and made her way to the local police station. A few coins were kept by the constabulary, who passed them on to the Royal Mint for testing. As Miss Tennent had expected, word came back confirming that they were forgeries.

The police decided that the best way of capturing the forgers was to lay a trap, and to wait for the young lad to return to the post office for his usual postal order. On 16 January 1930 the boy entered the post office as usual. At the counter he handed over four half crowns and one shilling, and asked for a ten shilling postal order. Two of the half crowns were rather shiny and bore the date 1920. The postal order was duly handed over.

Word was sent direct to the police, and they were able to follow the young lad from the shop. He made his way to a stairway in Union Place where he met with a man. The lad handed over the postal order. The police apprehended the man, but not without some effort. At length he was taken to the nearby Gayfield Police

Station and placed in a cell. During interviews he refused to identify himself, and a search of his clothing turned up a number of other coins, similar to the fraudulent ones that had been passed to the post office. Eventually the man revealed his name as James Steele.

The police made their way to Steele's flat, and during a search of the rooms discovered a locked box. In it were dies that had been used to make the counterfeit coins. In Robert Ramsay's room were discovered a number of forged half crowns.

From the flat in Caledonian Road the police made their way to the workshop in Murieston Crescent Lane. Once inside, they discovered many machines and pieces of equipment that had been used in the manufacture of the coins. So numerous was the equipment that it took the police two days to empty the workshop and take the evidence away. The equipment included a puncheon, four dies, an electric typing machine, a rolling machine, an edging machine, a charcoal stove, an annealing box, electro-plating tanks, frames, a hydraulic press, and an ejecting machine. These had been adapted and were used to impress the appearance of a current half-crown piece.

Ramsay and Steele were arrested and held in prison, awaiting trial. They appeared before Sheriff C.H. Brown at Edinburgh Sheriff Court on Tuesday 11 February 1930. Dugald Maclean, the men's solicitor, tendered a plea of guilty, subject to a few minor alterations to one of the dates. The sheriff intimated that as the charges were so serious, he would have to remit the case to the High Court for sentencing. This took place at the High Court in Edinburgh on 21 February 1930, when they pled guilty to the three charges that had been read out:

1. That between 28 May 1927 and 17 January 1930, in premises at Murieston Crescent Lane and in a house at 13 Caledonian Road, they had equipment used for counterfeiting.
2. That during the same period falsely made and counterfeited 1350 coins intended to resemble and pass for half crowns.

3. That on various dates within that period, and in particular on January 16 1930, in the sub post office at 3 Elm Row, Edinburgh, and elsewhere in Edinburgh, Glasgow and other parts of Scotland, they tendered counterfeit coins resembling half crown pieces.

According to the Royal Mint, who were involved in proving that the coins were counterfeit, the quality of the money that Ramsay and Steele had produced was of the highest standard, one of the best ever reproductions they had ever come across. The value of the coins that they were known to have produced was just over £168, which at today's prices would be in the region of £6,000–7,000. No doubt there were many other coins produced that the court had no evidence of.

The Lord Justice Clerk informed the two men that the first two charges read out to them were of such gravity that they could be sentenced to life imprisonment. He stated that the case 'was a deplorable one', as the men were obviously extremely talented. However, he decided that they should be imprisoned for three years.

For 30 years the story was thought to have ended there. However, on 18 November 1964 the police arrived at James Steele's home once again. He was an elderly man of 80 by this time and lived with his sister Lily. Steele's heart jumped when he answered the door to two policemen, but he calmed down when they informed him that they were making inquiries regarding the noise from a neighbouring joiner's workshop. Steele then invited them in, but it turned out that the door they had come to was the wrong one.

What happened in Steele's flat is not known, but when the two policemen were there it was discovered that Steele was still forging coins. In his bedroom the police found presses, dies, powder and other counterfeiting equipment. Again he was arrested, and charged with counterfeiting coins between the dates 1 April 1958 and 18 November 1964. It was reckoned that he had produced more than 14,000 florins (or ten-pence pieces) between those days.

Steele appeared at the Sheriff Court in Edinburgh on 8 December 1964. Again he pled guilty to the charge. Sheriff W. Ross McLean QC decided that the case should be remitted to the High Court for sentencing. On 10 December Steele stood in the dock where the Senior Advocate Depute, F.W.F. O'Brien, informed the court that his forgeries had again been of the best quality. The Royal Mint informed the court that the standard was extremely high and would easily deceive the general public and banks. In fact, the Mint had not seen counterfeits of such a good quality for many years.

Defending Steele was Nicholas Fairbairn. He informed the court that Steele was a single man who had previously worked at Miller's Foundry in the city's Abbeyhill, before retiring in 1955 following an accident. He failed to get another job as an engineer, and for a time had worked as a joiner. He had to survive on a pension, which was insufficient to keep him in his home. To make ends meet he had resorted to counterfeiting coins. To do this he purchased strips of metal at ten shillings each. These he took home and made into 40 high-quality two-shilling coins. The charge had been for making £1,400 worth of coins, but Steele had to purchase raw materials at £400 with which to make them.

Steele had made the coins himself, and nobody had assisted him in passing them into general circulation. His sister, Lily, was unaware of what her brother was doing, thinking that he spent time in his room making model railways and using photographic equipment, which were his two hobbies.

Lord Grant, the Lord Justice Clerk, informed Steele that according to the act under which he had been charged, he was due to sentence him for a minimum of three years. However, he had the power to change the sentence due to mitigating circumstances, and in view of his age, decided that a sentence of two years would suffice. Steele later submitted an appeal, but this was turned down on 22 December 1964.

# 10

# *German Atrocity Letters: Kate Hume*

The publication of the *Dumfries and Galloway Standard* on Wednesday 16 September 1914 caused a major sensation throughout Dumfries, a small southern Scottish town. Britain was at war with Germany and men were being called up to fight, women were being trained in new jobs, and families were waiting desperately for each post to receive letters from their loved ones.

The newspaper published two letters that had been received by a girl in the town giving news of her sister, who had been tortured and murdered by the Germans. The first read:

> 6th Sept.
> Dear Kate,
> This is to say Goodbye. Have not long to live. Hospital has been set on fire. Germans cruel. A man here has had head cut off, and my right breast taken away.
> Give my love to ————. Goodbye.
> Grace, X.

The second letter was longer, and was from a friend of Grace's, detailing what had happened to her:

Vilvorde, near Brussels

To Miss Hume,

I have been asked by your sister, Nurse Grace Hume, to hand the enclosed letter to you. My name is Nurse Mullard, and I was with your sister when she died. Our camp hospital at Vilvorde was burned to the ground, and out of 1,517 men and 23 nurses only 19 nurses were saved, but 149 men managed to get clear away. I expect to pass through Dumfries about the 15th September, but am writing this in case I should not see you. Your sister gave me your address, so, as I know Dumfries well, I shall send it to your office, if I do not see you.

As there is a shortage of nurses at Inverness, 15 of us are to be sent there. Grace requested me to tell you that her last thoughts were of Andrew and you, and that you were not to worry over her as she would be going to meet 'her Jock'. These were her words. She endured great agony in her last hour. One of the soldiers (our men) caught two German soldiers in the art of cutting off her left breast, her right one having been already cut off. They were killed instantly by our soldier.

Grace managed to scrawl this enclosed note before I found her. We can all say that your sister was a heroine. As she was a 'loose nurse' – that is, she was out on the fields looking for wounded soldiers – and on one occasion, when bringing in a wounded soldier, a German attacked her. She threw the soldier's gun at him and shot him with her rifle. Of course, all nurses here are armed. I have just received word this moment to pack for Scotland, so will try and get this handed to you as there is no post from here, and we are making the best of a broken down wagon truck for shelter. Will give you fuller details when I see you. We are all quite safe here now, as there have been reinforcements.

I am, yours sincerely,

J.M. Mullard, nurse, Royal Irish Troop. 7th September.

(Am not allowed to say which special troop)

Grace's father, Andrew Hume, who still lived in the town with his family, did not believe the information that was contained in the letters and he was convinced that they were a fabrication. On 13 September he contacted the editor of the *Standard,* William Dickie, to let him know of his concerns, and requested that the letters should not be published. The editor, however, felt that the shorter letter appeared genuine, but agreed that the long letter appeared to have been written by 'an excitable person'.

Mr Hume had also written to the War Office to find out if the story of his daughter's death was true, but had received no reply as yet. He was asked by the editor why he thought the letters were false and, if they were, then did he know who could have played such a hoax on him?

The town was in uproar over the atrocities that had befallen one of Dumfries' daughters and word spread and reached Grace Hume, who was still alive and living in Huddersfield. On 15 September 1914 she sent a telegram to the *Standard* to inform the paper that the story of her murder was untrue, and requested that the telegram should be publicly displayed in one of the newspaper office's windows so that the public could read this for themselves. Grace's telegram was displayed in the window of the newspaper offices on 16 September 1914, the day of publication.

Andrew Hume wrote back to his daughter, and she replied that she was sorry that there had been a lot of upset over the story, and that her father had been made miserable as a result of both this and the supposed reporting of her death. Grace continued, stating that she had no idea how the story could have originated, claiming that it was a complete mystery. She also confirmed that she neither knew nor had heard of a nurse named Mullard.

Grace also sent a postcard to Kate, in which she wrote, 'Dear Kate, Just received news of my own murder in Belgium. Can you give me particulars of the person calling herself Nurse Mullard?'

Inquiries in the town were commenced, and the route taken by the letters in reaching the newspaper office was traced backward.

Soon it became apparent that the source of the letters was Grace's sister, Kate, who worked in the town as an office clerkess.

Robert Laidlaw, who was the sub-editor of the *Standard,* had been sent to speak with Kate Hume on 16 September to try to find out a bit more about the letters. He asked how she got them, and was informed that Nurse Mullard had passed them to her. Laidlaw then went to Kate's father and asked to see the telegram he had received from Grace. He then returned to Kate's lodgings and told her that she must have been tricked, and that her sister was in fact alive and well. Kate replied, 'Well, I would like to think it is true, but I cannot believe it.' As far as she was concerned, the telegram her father had received must have been a forgery.

As time passed, it became obvious that Kate Hume had written the letters herself. She was arrested by the police and taken into custody, where she was held for 13 weeks prior to being taken to the High Court of Justiciary in Edinburgh and tried before the Lord Justice General on Monday 28 December 1914. Standing in the dock, the young woman wore a black hat and was dressed in a long blue coat adorned with a black fur necklet. It was reported that, even although she was just 17 years of age, she retained a perfectly calm composure throughout the hearing.

The charge was read out:

> . . . that between 4 August and 11 September 1914, the accused had, firstly, concocted and fabricated a letter bearing to be written to her and signed by her sister, Grace Hume, 62 Trinity Street, Huddersfield, the letter and signature 'Grace' being forged by her, and secondly, concocted and fabricated a letter bearing to be written to her from Vilvorde, near Brussels, and signed 'J.M. Mullard', the letter and signature being forged by her, and on 11 September, at the Old House, inferred the letters as genuine by handing them to Agnes Jane MacMinn, and on 14 September, by the hands of Robina MacMinn, daughter of Agnes Jane MacMinn, delivered them to Edward Hollingsworth Whitehead, newspaper

reporter, 7 Howgate Street, Maxwelltown, for publication as genuine letters in the Dumfries and Galloway Standard, Dumfries, and the letters were published in that newspaper, and all this she did with the intent of alarming and annoying the lieges, and in particular her father, Andrew Hume, and her stepmother, Alice Mary Hume, residing at 42 George Street, Dumfries.

In court, representing the Crown, were the Lord Advocate and Mr Morton, Advocate-Depute. Representing Hume were Mr Wilson and Mr W. J. Robertson. When asked how she pled to the charge read out in court, Kate responded by stating that she was 'Not Guilty'.

Mr Crole, the Clerk of Justiciary, informed the court that a special plea of defence had been lodged on behalf of the girl. It was claimed that at the time the alleged offence had been committed, Kate Hume's mind was so unbalanced that she could not, and did not, understand exactly what she was doing, and as a result was not fully responsible for her actions.

The first to be called as a witness for the Crown was Kate's father, Andrew Hume, who was 50 years of age. He was a music teacher, and lived in a sandstone building at the corner of George and Castle Streets in Dumfries. He related some of the family history to the court, setting the background to Kate's life. He explained that his first wife had died in 1906, leaving him with four children, Nellie, Grace, who was a nurse in Huddersfield, Kate, who stood in the dock, and a son, Andrew, who was still attending school. They had had a second son, John, who was drowned at the age of 21 when the *Titanic* sank in 1912. John had been a successful musician and played the violin in the band on board the doomed ship. His body was later recovered and is now buried in Fairview Cemetery, Halifax, Nova Scotia. He was the 'our Jock' referred to in the letter purporting to have been written by Nurse Mullard. Andrew continued by informing the court that he had married again in 1907, to Alice Mary.

Grace, the father continued, had left home a year or so after he had re-married, moving to Huddersfield where she worked as a nurse. She often returned to Dumfries for holidays. In July 1914 she returned to Dumfries for a break, but decided to give up working in Huddersfield, lodging in the town for ten days.

Kate had moved out of the family home on 7 August whilst her father was in Moffat on business, finding lodgings in the town with the MacMinn family at the Old House. Andrew Hume was not to see his daughter Kate from that time until after the letters had appeared in the newspaper.

Andrew Hume told the court that the letters looked to him as being more like his daughter Kate's handwriting than Grace's. He told the court that following the drowning of John, Kate had suffered some periods of depression, the two of them being more like friends than brother and sister. Both were talented musically, and this talent had passed like a vein through the family. Indeed, his grandfather had written the new versions of the tunes to Robert Burns' 'Afton Water' and 'The Emigrant's Farewell'. He had also written a number of tunes to the psalms. Kate had been musically talented herself, and he had high hopes for her.

Following Hume's second wedding, his new wife and Kate had fallen out on a number of occasions. Kate was growing fast, and wanted more freedom than her stepmother was willing to give. Kate enjoyed going out at night, though her father admitted that she was 'rather backward or childish for her years'. Though they had argued at times, there were no major differences between Kate and her stepmother. Nevertheless, she described Kate as headstrong, and Kate had moved out to give herself more liberty.

Andrew Hume told the court something of his daughter Grace's life. He did not think that it was possible that she could be a nurse at the front of the battle lines as she was uncertificated. In any case she had not informed him that she was going to help out at the front line. As a consequence of this he reckoned that there was no truth in the letters in the paper, and that they must have been made up. He did not think that his daughter Kate was capable of such a fraud. His second wife added to the reasons why they doubted the authenticity of the letters. She felt that Grace was insufficiently experienced to serve in the trenches, she was unable to ride on horseback, which the letter implied she could, and she had never before shot a gun.

Agnes MacMinn, Kate's landlady, was called into the witness box. She told the court that on Friday 11 September Kate Hume had arrived back at the lodging house between 11 a.m. and 12 a.m. This, she related, was an unusual time for her to return, being rather early. Kate ran in tears to the kitchen crying as she told her, 'Oh, Mrs MacMinn. Grace is dead!' She then handed over the two letters. Kate then sat at the kitchen table and wept uncontrollably.

Mrs MacMinn consoled Kate, calming her down, gradually eliciting the story from her. Kate said that Nurse Mullard had arrived at her place of work and handed over the two letters. One of these had been from her sister, Grace, the other was written by Nurse Mullard, to be given to Kate if she had not been able to make the journey to Dumfries and find her. Mrs MacMinn comforted the girl, and due to her reaction and the appearance of the letters, assumed that they were genuine. Agnes MacMinn and her daughter spent some time with Kate, but each time that they left her alone, she burst into tears again.

Word reached the *Standard* office of the letters, and a reporter, Edward Whitehead, was sent to the home of Mrs MacMinn on 14 September. He asked to speak with Kate, but the landlady told him that she was unwell. He then requested to see the letters. Robina, the daughter, went to Kate and told her about the reporter. She was given permission to take them from her handbag and pass them over, so long as they were returned to her.

When Kate's employer, James Campbell, was questioned, he told the court that Kate had been an intelligent and competent worker as a bookkeeper and clerkess in his business for the past two and a half years. On the night of 11 September he found Kate in the office, and she told him that Grace was dead, showing him the letters. He thought that the paper they were written on was the same as that used in his office, with the letterhead ripped off. He also felt that the handwriting was definitely that of Kate's. Evidence came from an employee of a Dumfries printer, Thomas Hunter, who confirmed that the watermark in the paper used for the letters was the same as that used in the letterheadings produced by his company for Anderson & Munro Ltd, Kate's employer.

The supposed murder victim was called into the witness box. Grace Hume, who was 22 years of age, informed the court that she had been a nurse in Oldham for 18 months, prior to moving to Huddersfield. She first discovered the story that she was supposed to have been the victim of German atrocities, resulting in her own murder, when she read it in an English newspaper, which had reproduced it from the *Standard*.

Further evidence in the court was supplied by Sir W.S. Haldane, Crown Agent, who informed the jury that he had investigated as far as was possible whether there was a real Nurse Mullard, but so far he had drawn a blank. William Smith, a handwriting expert from Edinburgh, had studied the letters as well as the handwriting of Grace and Kate, and reckoned that the letters were in fact the work of the accused.

Kate Hume was then called into the witness box. She explained that she did not get on too well with her stepmother, and that she had suffered depression following the death of her brother in the *Titanic* disaster. She had been close to Grace, but once she had moved out into lodgings she had not heard from her, despite writing a few times. Gradually the thought that she had moved to the battlefront crossed her mind and, on the day that the letters were written, she admitted reading some of the newspapers at her work, in which tales of German atrocities were recounted. Whether or not all of this had affected her and caused her to write the letters she did not know. Reported in the newspapers, she continued:

Ever since the war began her nerves had been greatly worked upon, and she believed that her sister had gone to the front and been killed. She remembered writing the letters, but she did not know what caused her to write them. She certainly had no intention of creating a sensation, or of harming her father or step-mother . . . she said she fancied her sister in her last moments writing to her in that way. She did not know what had led her to write them, but she was thinking at the time of her having had to leave home, of the *Titanic* disaster, and of the brutalities the Germans were practising. It was her full belief her sister was at the front because she had received no word from her.

When asked where the name for Nurse Mullard had come from, she reckoned that she must have thought of it from the surname of another Dumfries victim of the *Titanic* shipwreck. This was Thomas Mullin, who was a third-class steward on board the ship. In Dumfries' Dock Park an obelisk had been erected in memory of the town's two *Titanic* victims.

The trial closed when the evidence had been presented, and the court adjourned. On the following day the court resumed, and evidence from doctors stated that Kate was not insane at the time she wrote the letters, nor at present. The jury retired at 2.50 p.m. and within 15 minutes returned with their verdict. They found Kate Hume guilty of having written the letters as charged, but as she had not been aware that she was committing a crime when she did so, they recommended that the judge be lenient with her.

The Lord Justice General informed Kate Hume that he was willing to accept what the jury had said, and as she had already spent upwards of three months in prison, and due to the fact that previously she had been of good character, and as she was still young, he would find her guilty, but would release her on probation.

The court erupted in applause.

# 11

# 'Unheard-of impositions':
# Archibald MacNab,
# 17th Chief of MacNab

The death of Francis MacNab, 16th Chief of the MacNabs, in 1816 saw the end of one of the last great characters of Highland Scotland. Despite the Battle of Culloden in 1746 bringing a close to the Jacobite movement, and the gradual integration of Highlanders into the British way of life, Francis MacNab had lived very much in the old manner. He retained the traditions of chiefdom until his death, becoming something of a celebrity and an object of fun for his eccentric and outmoded way of life.

Francis MacNab was taken to the traditional burial island of the MacNabs, Innis Buidhe, which is surrounded by the waters of the River Dochart, at Killin in Perthshire. His funeral was something of a spectacle, the burial of one of the last great chiefs attracting the attention of the press of the day. A large oak coffin (for Francis was a very tall man) was borne by clansmen along the streets of Killin to the little island at the head of Loch Tay, where he was ceremoniously buried with his ancestors. He had never married, but had numerous illegitimate children.

The new chief, his nephew Archibald MacNab, soon discovered

how large his new patrimony was. The extent of the clan homelands was just 25 acres located around the clan seat, Kinnell House, near Killin, as well as two small farms let to tenants. The whole estate brought an income of just £1,000 per annum, whereas the debts he had inherited from his uncle were estimated at around £35,000, perhaps around £2 million today. The honour of being a clan chief was beginning to evaporate!

Archibald MacNab was born in 1778, the son of Dr Robert MacNab (d. 1814) and grandson of John MacNab, 15th Chief. He was trained as a lawyer in London. MacNab spent much of his time in the bars of London, as well as in Paris, where it is known that he frequented brothels.

Archibald MacNab married Margaret Robertson, daughter of a Writer to the Signet, or solicitor, in Edinburgh. She was something of a catch. They were unlucky in raising a family, for five of their six children were to die in infancy, or at least at a young age. William died aged 20, Alexander aged 10, Margaret aged 18, and two other children within a short time of their birth. Only Sarah Anne survived into full adulthood.

Inheriting Kinnell and the MacNab debts at the age of 28 changed MacNab. He began drinking heavily, and he seemed to care nothing about the money that he owed. Indeed, Dugald MacNab, an elderly retainer who had worked for his uncle, encouraged him to spend as he wished, ignoring his creditors, just as the last chief would have done.

However, MacNab's training as a lawyer meant that he knew he couldn't ignore the debts forever. He managed to sell some of the lands in 1823, but a writ of foreclosure was issued for the remaining debts. The king's officers would be coming sometime to arrest him for his debts, and he didn't want to face them. He decided that he would have to do something serious.

Two options lay before him – suicide or disappearance. He decided on the latter, so he got up from his bed during the early hours of the morning and dressed himself in his plaid. He made his way down from the bedroom of Kinnell House and out into the yard. MacNab then went to the home of Dugald MacNab and roused him from his slumbers. The two men disappeared from Perthshire, never to return.

Whether MacNab knew what was about to happen the following morning or not is unknown, but on that day the officers arrived with a warrant for his arrest. They appear to have forced an entry into the house, only to discover a cowering family, MacNab's wife and child crying together, aware that Francis had left them.

MacNab and Dugald made their way to London where they purchased a passage to Canada. The journey took one month in those days, during which time MacNab revealed to the other emigrants that he was the chief of a Scottish clan. That he was penniless was conveniently forgotten. On his arrival at Canada he marched down the gangway with the air of a king – dressed in his tartan plaid and his bonnet sporting three eagle feathers to signify his position as chief of his clan.

Archibald MacNab travelled to Montreal where he met up with Bishop Alexander MacDonell. MacDonell had previously taken over a large extent of Canadian land and settled many MacDonell clansmen there, taking them from Glengarry in Inverness-shire to a new life. MacNab explained that he would like the lease of a tract of Canadian land, and that he would also bring clansmen from the MacNab homelands of Perthshire to settle it. MacDonell advised MacNab that he should contact Sir Peregrine Maitland, Governor of Canada at the time, who would be the most likely person to help him.

Maitland assisted MacNab in drawing up a petition which was presented to the government. In it he requested that a stretch of land should be given to him to allow him to grant blocks of 100 acres to each of the families he would bring from Scotland. The titles to the lands would be held by MacNab and not granted to the settlers until such time as they earned a certificate proving good citizenship. The new settlers, according to MacNab, would be brought to Canada at his own expense and all that he would take from the scheme was a figure from the settlers that would reimburse his expenses in transporting them across the Atlantic Ocean.

At first the Canadian government turned down MacNab's proposals, for they seemed to be indicating that the grant of land was being given to MacNab, who would then become landlord to the clansmen that he would bring across the ocean at no expense to himself. However, on 5 November 1823 a document was drawn up which apparently gifted MacNab 80,000 acres of land to populate. The government was under the impression that MacNab would supervise the new settlers for 12 months, after which they would be given the title deeds to 100 acres of land each. These settlers would refund MacNab any money that he loaned them in the meantime, along with interest, and had the right to repay both capital and interest in a single payment within one year. However, MacNab's legal mind spotted a flaw in the whole system, and he failed to pass on much of the information of the agreement to the settlers.

The lands granted to MacNab lay on the southern shores of Lac de Chats, on the west side of the River Madawaska, in the province of Ontario. There, on a low hill overlooking the lake he built a large log cabin which was named Kinnell Lodge, in honour of the ancestral estate back in Scotland. The township that he was to establish was named Macnab.

With the land tied up, MacNab contacted a friend back in Scotland to arrange for the transportation of families for the new settlement. MacNab's cousin, Dr Francis Buchanan Hamilton of Leny, was asked to select 20 families who were keen to emigrate to Canada. These families would form the basis of a larger community that would be built up on the Macnab lands. MacNab also told Hamilton that within a few years he would have made sufficient funds to return to Scotland and pay off the MacNab debts, and even extend the MacNab estate in Perthshire – 'Now I am in a fine way to redeem the estate at home, and in a few years will return after having established a name in Canada, and founded a transatlantic colony of the clan.'

Hamilton was able to get the 20 families that MacNab requested. They all agreed to sign the bond that MacNab had drawn up, in which they agreed to pay him the sum of £36 to cover transportation costs and other expenses. The initial cost of board on a sailing ship from Scotland to Canada was only £3 each, and this figure was paid for by Hamilton.

Eighty-four men, women and children stepped on board the *Niagara* at Greenock on 19 April 1825 to begin a journey that would change their lives. They spent 38 days on board the ship, being tossed by the waves as they crossed the ocean. Many of them had never seen the sea before, let alone sailed on it. When Canada was sighted in the distance they were delighted, and soon they sailed up the St Lawrence estuary and reached port at Quebec. On the quayside stood Archibald MacNab, dressed in full Highland regalia with his chief's eagle feathers. By his side was MacNab's piper, playing a welcoming tune.

The new settlers gathered around MacNab, who proudly welcomed them to Canada. He gathered in the bonds that they had signed, though two men refused to hand these over. They were both school teachers who, having more education than the others, would not pass over the paper until they had taken possession of their land.

The MacNab settlers were transported by barge up the St Lawrence towards Montreal, followed by the Ottawa River for three days before landing once more. With their baggage in tow, they commenced marching across country, through extensive swamplands. The marshes were so large that it took 11 days to cross them, after which the landscape changed. Soon they were in dense forest lands, and a further 17 days of travelling brought them to the edge of Lac de Chats, 200 miles from Quebec. On 23 June

1825 they spotted a largish clearing, with Kinnell Lodge standing proudly on its knoll.

At Kinnell Lodge the new settlers were treated to a grand meal. A deer had been killed and cooked over the fire, and it was now being served with whisky. In good spirits, the settlers retired for the evening. On the following day, MacNab addressed them. He informed them that they would each receive a grant of 100 acres, for which no rent was payable for the first three years. After that they would pay either him, or failing that his heirs, one bushel of wheat or Indian corn per annum for every cleared acre of ground, *for ever*. Again, almost all of the incomers signed up to what appeared to be a great deal – but MacNab was in fact taking a rent for ground that had been granted free by the Governor of Canada.

The settlers began to take on their land in earnest. Their first task was to cut down the trees that covered each farm, and this was to prove quite troublesome, for few of them had any experience in timber felling. As they cut down their first few trees they soon realised the massive task that faced them. Even after a few acres or so were cut down, the ground was still too poor to grow any crops, without clearing of roots and levelling out land to create fields.

Despite promising a year's provisions, MacNab didn't supply this, resulting in much hardship in the community. With no income to speak of, the settlers asked MacNab for a loan to buy food and clothing. Having no funds of his own, he refused their request, telling them that they should be grateful to him for giving them such an opportunity. The settlers then asked if they could have permission to work for others, and MacNab agreed to this. Soon most of the men were away working elsewhere, either as labourers on neighbouring building projects, or else as lumberjacks in commercial forestry enterprises.

Despite leaving the settlers with little means of keeping themselves for the foreseeable future, MacNab then added fuel to the fire by announcing that all of the timber they had cut down actually belonged to him. He informed them that they were not allowed to sell it, and that he could collect all the trees they had cut down and sell the timber himself.

Not all of the settlers agreed to this, and Alexander Miller, one of the school teachers who had refused to hand over the settlement bond, sold his timber to a neighbour. MacNab reported this to the Canadian authorities, and the neighbour who bought the timber was fined. Miller was arrested and placed in gaol, under the charge of owing MacNab £80. A few of his friends paid his bail but these guarantors were subject to MacNab's ire, and had to pay £50 in costs.

One of the settlers wrote to the Governor of Canada to complain about MacNab's treatment of them, and of the terms in their bonds. MacNab reckoned that it had been Alexander MacNab that had sent the complaint, and he replied to him:

Alexander MacNab, degraded clansman;
You are accused to me by Sir John Colbourne, of libel, sedition and high treason. You will forthwith appear before me at my house of Kinnell and there make a submission; and if you show a contrite and repentant spirit, and confess your faults against me, your legitimate chief, and your crime against His Majesty King George, I will intercede for your pardon.
Your offended chief,
MacNab.

Timber rights became a major difficulty for the settlers. MacNab had now illegally sold all the timber on the large grant of land to two brothers. They had set up a sawmill near to the mouth of the River Madawaska, at a place that MacNab was to name Arnprior, after the home of his mother in Stirlingshire.

Back in Scotland things were moving on apace. In 1828 sheriff officers evicted MacNab's wife and daughter from Kinnell House and sold the property and land to assist in the payment of MacNab's debts, leaving his wife and daughter homeless.

In 1830 an inspection was made of the settlement by a number of government representatives. They found that MacNab was charging interest at an exorbitant rate, and that anyone who wished to redeem their bonds found the cost prohibitive. The settlement also seemed to be progressing at a far slower rate than equivalent settlements elsewhere in Canada, MacNab taking too much out of the scheme, whereas other settlements often ploughed the profits back into the development.

Undaunted by the poor publicity that the inspection had brought him, and which reached back to Scotland, MacNab decided that he would take on a further 5,000 acres. He contacted Hamilton back in Scotland to find him more settlers, but he refused, having heard of the scandal of MacNab's terms. Instead, MacNab went to Montreal, where he awaited the arrival of ships carrying new settlers, offering them bonds for farms. The émigrés signed these rather too quickly, not realising that they could get grants of land direct from the Canadian government, and also financial help to boot. In this way MacNab swindled a further set of 40 families, who had come from the Blair Atholl district in Perthshire.

MacNab's handling of the Canadian estates put a great strain on the relationship between himself and his retainer, Dugald MacNab. Dugald eventually left him, finding employment elsewhere. MacNab then started a liaison with his housekeeper, Catherine Fisher. They both turned to whisky, and often when the settlers asked for an audience with their landlord, they were shown into the bedroom at Kinnell Lodge, where MacNab and Catherine were often lying in bed together in a drunken stupor.

The relationship between MacNab and his tenants never improved and he was accused many times of vindictive actions against them. Any tenant who was due to be evicted, for whatever reason, he usually left alone until the winter months, when the eviction would be harder on them. He often employed men on schemes at the opposite end of the settlement from their homes, making them travel excessive distances for work. Many of the projects he started were abandoned halfway through, and the men were forced to build new projects to replace them.

One of MacNab's great schemes commenced in 1836. Using the old clan method of raising the clansmen for battle, he sent round the fiery cross and ordered that they should meet to receive instructions. With the men all gathered expectantly, he announced that he was abandoning Kinnell Lodge, and that a new house would be built on the shores of Lake Waba, eight miles distant. As chief, he expected every clansman to supply him with one month's worth of labour. There was a great outcry against this, but MacNab's fiery temper and personality was such that they submitted to carrying out the work.

By 1839 Canada had become a more settled country. A new government had raised standards considerably, and many corrupt and nepotistic officials had been forced from office. A report was issued by Francis Allen, a Crown agent, on the township of Macnab, in which the situation was severely damned. In it Archibald MacNab was accused of oppression and of fraud, for making his tenants pay for land that was theirs by right.

Realising that it might be time to give up his part in running the estate, MacNab offered to return all rights to Macnab to the Canadian government in exchange for a payment of £9,000 (or around £500,000 today). The government considered the deal, but questioned many of Macnab's costs and, as he was unable to prove his expenses, nothing came of the claim.

On 3 June 1840 MacNab's tenants sent a petition to the Canadian government in which they claimed:

That for the last fifteen years your Petitioners, as settlers under the Laird of MacNab, have been persecuted, harassed with law-suits, threatened with deprivation of their lands, and subjected to threats by the MacNab, of being driven from their present locations by the Government, for disobedience to the Chief.

That the said Chief has impoverished many families, and completely ruined those of Alex. MacNab, Peter and John McIntyre, whom he brought to Canada.

That there are now sixteen families still remaining in the township whom his friends sent out to Canada as settlers under him, who are willing to pay to the Chief any reasonable sum as passage-money, that Your Excellency in Council may deem just to impose; but on the other hand your Petitioners have hitherto resisted, and will continue constitutionally to resist any attempts to impose the feudal system of the Dark Ages upon Your Petitioners or their descendants.

In the meantime, the net closing in on him, MacNab continued to harass his tenants. He demolished a meal mill at Lake Waba, resulting in the settlers having to travel 16 miles to the next nearest mill. MacNab then built a new saw mill of his own, but located this on the 4th concession line, right in the middle of the public highway between the present towns of Renfrew and Pakenham, resulting in the settlers having to build a new road around the mill.

A John Paris moved into the area and set up a new grist mill on church lands which was ready for operation by the autumn. MacNab, however, placed every obstruction in Paris' way to prevent the mill from being built, and forbade his tenants from using it. He even went as far as raising the dam upstream to deny the new mill a suitable supply of water.

MacNab was summoned to court to face charges of being a public nuisance. He was found guilty and fined.

With the tide turning against him, the final straw came when his former retainer, Dugald MacNab passed on the original agreement between the Canadian authorities and MacNab, in which the terms of the land grant were laid out, to the *Toronto*

*Examiner*. In November 1840 the newspaper exposed MacNab as a fraudster, detailing the 'unheard of impositions' that the settlers in the township of Macnab had to endure.

MacNab fought back, however, and took the newspaper to court in Toronto on a libel charge. The court sat in April 1842 and found in MacNab's favour. He was awarded the princely sum of £5 for loss of character!

In a final attempt at asserting his authority, MacNab carried out an eviction that had been held in abeyance. MacNab, the Sheriff Depute and a third man went to the home of Duncan MacNab. He was away working, and only his wife and children were at home. The Sheriff Depute carried out his official duties, removing the family from the house, and then left. MacNab then ordered the third man to remove the family and their possessions to the concession line, whereupon he set fire to the house. Mrs MacNab spotted the smoke rising, and suddenly realised that two of her children were missing. In a frantic moment she ran into the burning barn where she found them hiding in the straw, frightened by the spectacle of their eviction. Mrs MacNab managed to rescue them, and it was noted that had she been two minutes later they would have perished in the flames.

With the Canadian population now against him, MacNab made a sudden exit from the township he had established. He moved to Hamilton, in Ontario, where he was forced to live in virtual poverty in a wooden shanty house for just over two years.

Stories of MacNab's treatment of the Canadian settlers reached Scotland, where his wife heard them. Although she had not seen him for 28 years, she still had some feelings for him, and did not wish him to live in such squalor. She organised a search for him, and he was willing to accept her charity. Accordingly, in 1848 she paid for his return to Scotland, though she did not wish him in her new home. Instead she purchased a house for him to live in, located on the mainland of Orkney. This was the White House of Breck, which stands at Rendall, 12 miles from Kirkwall, overlooking the Wide Firth. Prior to leaving North America, a daguerreotype picture of him was taken at Saratoga, in the United States.

MacNab lived much of the remainder of his life in Orkney. He was still addicted to drink, and still had delusions of his importance as clan chief, paying a local piper to come to his home on a regular basis to play the tune, 'The Gathering of Clan MacNab'. The clan that followed him was now gone, but he still had some pull with the ladies. Despite being over 70 years of age by this time, he enjoyed the favours of two local women who moved into the White House with him. Later on he met another woman, the daughter of an English ironmonger. They lived together for a while, she becoming pregnant by him. To avoid the scandal this would have created amongst the close-knit community of the Orkney Isles they moved to Paris. MacNab then left the mother of his illegitimate child and moved to Lannion, on the Côtes du Nord, in Brittany, France, on 12 August 1860. He died there and was buried in the local churchyard in an unmarked grave.

Archibald's first wife, Margaret, was still alive, as was their daughter, Sarah Anne (or Sophia Frances) MacNab. Margaret, died on 20 June 1868. The chiefship of the clan went into dispute, though Sarah was later recognised as the 18th Chief. When she died unmarried on 19 January 1894 the title of Clan Chief eventually settled on a branch of the family in Berkshire, whose descendants still hold the title.

# 12

# *The Old Boy at School: Brian MacKinnon*

It all started as a fairly normal day at work for Norman MacLeod, head teacher at Bearsden Academy, in the north-west of Glasgow. However, as the day progressed, it became apparent that things were taking an unusual turn, and within hours the world's media attention was focussed on the school. A full staff meeting was quickly arranged and the teachers filed into the assembly hall at the end of the day.

Mr MacLeod stood up at the front and began addressing the staff. He informed them that within the past couple of years there had been an impostor in the school, one who had enrolled and who had been taught in classes by a variety of teachers. However, it had now come to light that this pupil was not of school age, and that in fact he was 30 years old. The con had fooled him, too, MacLeod admitted, and there was a hint of humour in his voice when he held his hands up and admitted that they had all been taken in. MacLeod continued to explain why international news teams, such as ABC from the United States, were in the vicinity of the school grounds, looking for quotes, and he warned staff to be very wary of anything they said. One television news company even went to the bother of hiring a platform lorry, rather like a

Simon snorkel fire engine, so that it could obtain pictures looking into the school grounds.

The school pupil had arrived in 1993 and requested to be enrolled into the fifth year. There was nothing unusual in the request, and the school checked that the address he gave was bona fide, and did exist within the school's catchment area. He claimed that he was living with his grandmother, who was in fact his mother, and he had enrolled himself as she was unfit to visit the school. He also passed over documents that purported to be from his previous tutors, supposedly in Canada, which looked genuine to the staff. It was also noted by some that he often spoke with a Canadian or American accent. His name, Brandon Lee, was quite unusual in that it was the same name as the son of actor Bruce Lee, the famous martial arts film star, but over the years many pupils had passed through the school sharing the same names as famous footballers, actors and the like.

Brandon Lee was regarded by his teachers as something of a model pupil. He took part in many extra-curricular activities, and was particularly keen on acting. He played the role of Lieutenant Cable in the school performance of *South Pacific*, performing on stage with other senior pupils. Initially he shied away from acting in public, for fear of being rumbled by someone in the audience, but a persuasive teacher managed to get him to take on the part. He wrote articles for the school magazine, one of which was based on the relationship between a mother and her boyfriend.

In his studies Brandon Lee worked hard. He was desperate to become a doctor, and he selected subjects that would earn him a place at university. At the end of June 1994 he sat five Higher Grade examinations, in English, Maths, Biology, Chemistry and Physics, which he duly passed, all at 'A' grade.

Brandon Lee enrolled at Dundee University, where he was able to commence studying medicine. He still claimed to be a teenager, now 18 years of age, but for personal reasons he had to give up the course at the end of his first term. Nevertheless, he was due to return to university and continue studying in September 1995.

During the summer of 1995 Brandon and two girls who had been classmates of his at Bearsden went on holiday to Tenerife, staying in a flat at Playa de Las Americas. The girls had remained at Bearsden for a sixth year, but had now left. Whilst on the Spanish holiday island, Brandon Lee admitted to the girls, Sheila Loudon and Gillian McCallum, that his real name was Brian MacKinnon and that he was not really a teenager but was in fact 32. He admitted that he was really 30 whilst he was at Bearsden Academy and that he had conned the school to allow him to get another chance to return to university.

The girls and Brandon fell out regarding the situation and things became tense. In the morning he told them that he was going out for a walk, but instead he went to a travel agent and booked himself an early flight home. He returned to Scotland on 8 August, knowing to some extent that his deception could probably not be kept up much longer.

Another girl on the holiday, Nicola Walker, told her parents Lee's story when she returned, and soon tales of the double life of Brandon Lee were doing the rounds in Bearsden. A parent who had heard the rumours telephoned the head teacher, Norman MacLeod, to inform him. MacLeod regarded the story as rather unbelievable to start with, but decided to investigate just in case. In the school records he dug out the file for Brian MacKinnon and compared it with that of Brandon Lee. The pictures of the pupil were similar, apart from the age difference. MacLeod was able to track down Lee at his home and MacLeod invited him in for a talk.

Brandon Lee still maintained that he was not the same person as Brian MacKinnon, and explained to Mr MacLeod that he was going on holiday to Germany, and that he would prove that he was someone else when he returned. MacLeod told him that he would allow him the week to prove that he was indeed who he said he was, before passing on the information to Dundee University. However, MacLeod was not convinced by his story, and decided to inform the education department of what he had discovered. Before Brandon Lee was able to return from Germany, or wherever he was in hiding, perhaps falsifying certificates, the story broke.

Staff and pupils at the school were taken aback at the news. Some pupils did think when he first came to the school that he was older-looking, but they gradually accepted his appearance. Others noticed that he spoke in a more mature manner than most pupils, but this was put down to his life in Canada, where things may have been different. It was noted, however, that he still liked to laugh and joke about the same things as the rest of the senior pupils.

Some teaching staff who had been employed at Bearsden Academy over a lengthy period began to realise that they had taught him before, for as Brian Lachlan MacKinnon, born on 4 June 1963, he had attended the school from 1974 until 1980. Not one of them had realised that this was the same person. At that time he gained four Grade 'A' Higher passes and two at Grade 'B.'

After leaving school for the first time in 1980, Brian MacKinnon had enrolled in Glasgow University where he set out on a medical course. He worked hard on the course, continuing to study for three years, but eventually dropped out. He had failed his first year examinations, but passed the re-sits. During his second year he had taken ill, and was unable to complete the course. Nevertheless, the university allowed him to repeat the year, but he again failed the examinations and also the re-sits. The university then decided that he should not be allowed to continue his studies.

After a period he was able to return to Glasgow University and studied a science course, gaining an Honours Degree in 1989. His main subject was pathology. However, he did not return to find out his results, aware that the degree was still insufficient qualification to allow him to become a doctor, and thus he failed to graduate from the university.

Why he failed to graduate from university is a bit of a mystery, but it has been claimed that MacKinnon knew at the time that if he graduated his details would be added to the General Council Register. This would, to some extent, bar him from returning to university once more and from claiming grants towards the payment of his medical tuition fees, or from obtaining a maintenance allowance for his accommodation. By failing to graduate and returning as someone else, MacKinnon's chances of re-matriculating at university would be greater.

MacKinnon petitioned the senate of Glasgow University to allow him to return to his courses, but they turned him down. Letters from his mother were also unsuccessful. He wrote a standard letter to one member of the senate, but photocopied it 180 times and sent it to all members of the university senate, an action that was to lead to him being described as obsessive. He continued to send letters pleading to be allowed back on the course up until 1991.

Failing to graduate, Brian MacKinnon spent some time working out how he would be able to return to university to study medicine. At length his plan to return to school as someone else for one year and re-qualify was hatched, and so he enrolled at his old school as Brandon Lee.

Once MacKinnon's deceit was uncovered, Dundee University announced that he was to be suspended from the course. He had already completed part of his first year as an undergraduate between October and December, before pulling out. He wrote to the university claiming that his grandmother had died, before informing them that he was taking a year out for financial reasons. MacKinnon was due to return in October 1995. A spokesman reported, 'If he is prepared to lie his way onto a course, can he be trusted in such matters as writing prescriptions?' It was confirmed that although MacKinnon had not actually broken any law in returning to university, the authorities at Dundee were of the opinion that they would be unable to keep him on the course. Other students who had applied for the course but were unsuccessful chanced their luck and wrote or phoned the university to find out if they could take Lee's place!

When news of MacKinnon's deceit broke, he went into hiding. A media frenzy ensued, with tabloid and broadsheet newspaper reporters making their way to Bearsden to try to find him. Television crews and radio reporters all headed for the school, hoping to find someone who could give them any little extra snippet about him, or who could even be persuaded to tell them where he was hiding. He had told some friends that he was going to Germany for a week, but it was not known if this was true, or just a tale to help cover his tracks. Journalists from various tabloids set up camp outside the home of his mother, offering financial rewards to anyone with vital information. The American television network, ABC, made its way to Bearsden and was able to interview Norman MacLeod on the amazing story.

Within a few days Brian MacKinnon returned early from Germany and wrote to the Glasgow newspaper, *The Herald*. Despite the whirlwind of media speculators looking for his story, he decided to offer his story to *The Herald*, and for no fee. This was a result of *Herald* reporters having given fellow classmates a chance to put their side of the story to the paper, in which they supported MacKinnon, in an unsensational way. At 3.30 p.m. on Sunday 24 September Brian MacKinnon phoned the paper's newsroom and asked to speak to the news desk.

In his call he explained that he had planned the elaborate hoax as a means of getting back into university to study medicine after he had been 'robbed' of his place at Glasgow University the first time round. Unable to get another chance, MacKinnon had tried every avenue he could find to get a route back into university. All roads seemed to be closed so he even tried to enrol in a medical school in Canada, with no success.

Desperate to qualify as a doctor, MacKinnon then resorted to what he termed 'dishonest means'. He created two letters of introduction which allowed him to return to school, and he was amazed when he found that they worked and he was enrolled as a pupil. To try to make sure that the teachers at the school who had taught him the first time round were unlikely to spot that he was the same person, MacKinnon plucked his eyebrows and had his hair permed. He was very nervous when he turned up at school, knowing that he could be caught out at any moment, but he was able to fool the staff into enrolling him. In his initial interview he was asked by the teacher for his birth certificate, but then the teacher said, 'No, never mind. I believe you.'

At the back of MacKinnon's mind there was always the knowledge that he shouldn't really be back at his old school as an imposter, but he ignored this and concentrated on his studies. Even these he had to be careful about, for he found the Higher courses rather easy, and he had to make sure that he did not become regarded as something of a prodigy, winning prizes and dux medals. Any attention that he attracted might have blown his cover.

Only on a few occasions were there any hints that Brandon Lee was not all that he seemed. On one occasion he was talking with his friends at Bearsden Academy when he happened to mention that he remembered the death of Elvis Presley. As the king of rock and roll died in 1977, his fellow pupils wondered how a boy of 17 years would remember an incident that took place when he was only one year old. On another occasion a parcel was sent from Dundee University to Brandon Lee at his Bearsden address. His mother not being in, it was left with a neighbour. MacKinnon successfully managed to talk his way out of both incidents.

His mother, May MacKinnon, was under the impression that her son had returned to school as an adult learner, something that was encouraged by secondary schools. A retired psychiatric nurse, Mrs MacKinnon was 70 years of age when the tale of her son broke. She was adamant that she knew nothing of her son's double-life, and had recently endured the death of her husband from cancer. Brian MacKinnon also had a younger sister.

Prior to his real identity being revealed, MacKinnon knew that his time at Dundee University might soon be up anyway. Because MacKinnon had dropped out of his first year he had to re-enrol. However, the regulations covering enrolment had been tightened up since he dropped out. Dundee University requested that Brandon bring his birth certificate with him. With no genuine birth certificate as Brandon Lee, MacKinnon knew that his cover could soon be blown.

The media frenzy at MacKinnon's home in Bearsden's Stirling Drive forced him and his mother to temporarily move out. Newspapers proffered open chequebooks, hoping that it would persuade him to tell his side of the story, but he turned all offers down. MacKinnon sent letters of explanation to Dundee University, but these were passed on by a representative of *The Herald*, something the university found unacceptable. They cancelled his admission to the medical course.

On 27 September 1995 Brian MacKinnon was interviewed by Strathclyde Police at their Milngavie police station. They wished to see if there was any substance to some of the stories that had appeared in the newspapers. One of these was that he had been involved in a fight in a bar in Tenerife, but this had not been the case. After being questioned for one hour, he was released, no charge having been made. Another tale that went the rounds early on was that he had two passports, but he was able to confirm that he did not. The police had already made investigations at Glasgow Passport Office into whether there was a possibility that he did. MacKinnon also confirmed that during his first year at Dundee University he did not receive a grant of any kind, and so did not misuse public money.

The media often tracked MacKinnon down from that time onward, and in 1997 it was claimed by one newspaper that he was threatening to create yet another persona, in order to attempt a return to medical school. In the same year he wrote an autobiography that he published on his own website. Titled *Margin Walker*, MacKinnon negotiated with a publisher to get it into print. However, this plan was later abandoned when the book was discovered to contain libellous allegations against Glasgow and Dundee University medical faculties, as well as some of the pupils he had studied with at Bearsden the second time around. MacKinnon later also withdrew the autobiography from the internet.

Another tack MacKinnon followed was to take his case to the European Courts, claiming that Glasgow University had initially mistreated him by 'pre-emptorily excluding' him from studying medicine. However, in May 2001 the courts responded by stating that they could not take up his case as it occurred prior to the time when the court's jurisdiction came into force.

By July 2002 MacKinnon was forced into living in his own car, claiming that he was homeless and had little money. He told newspapers that he was still desperate to make it as a doctor, saying 'I'm still sharp, I'm still enthusiastic, I have a sense of vocation and I have the ability.'

MacKinnon's story grabbed the world's attention, and it still appears in lists of top hoaxes. Film producer Peter Broughan latched on to the tale and reckoned that it would make a great movie. He was able to secure £850,000 of lottery money and had lined up comic actor Alan Cumming to play MacKinnon in the film, to be titled *Younger than Springtime,* from the title of one of the songs in *South Pacific.* However, MacKinnon wanted the chance to play himself in the film, and he and Broughan squabbled over the rights. No other funds were forthcoming and Broughan decided to put the idea on hold. He was quoted as saying, 'We haven't been actively developing it for a while, which isn't to say it's entirely dead.'

# 13

# *The Laird of Drumblair:*
# *George Clifford Charles Williams*

There is a Strathspey tune entitled 'The Laird o' Drumblair' that was written sometime in the Victorian period by the self-styled Strathspey king, James Scott Skinner (1843–1927), who was the leading performer of Scottish fiddle music in his time. The Laird in question was William M.F. MacHardy, who lived at Drumblair House, which lies in the Aberdeenshire countryside, about seven miles east of Huntly. MacHardy was a successful engineer, having made over £100,000 in projects in South Africa, before retiring to Aberdeenshire. He was a friend and patron of Skinner, and MacHardy allowed him the use of a cottage on the estate rent-free.

The music for the tune came to Skinner one night when he was lying in bed, thinking of how generous MacHardy was to him. Suddenly a melody came into his head, and he jumped out of bed to find a piece of paper, on which to write it down. The only thing that came to hand was the wrapping paper of a bar of soap. Undaunted, Skinner jotted down his tune. His wife watched as he did this, and on being told what he was going to do with it, protested, 'Ye're no' gaun tae send that awfu'-like paper tae the laird. He'll jist licht his pipe wi' it!' However, Skinner did, and so impressed was MacHardy with the tune that from that time onward he sent a cheque to Skinner every Christmas. The tune, which is still a popular one, is often performed by expert fiddlers at various competitions.

The Laird of Drumblair that this chapter refers to was a different person, one whose background and benefactions were not so honourable.

Lieutenant Colonel George Hanbury Williams drove through the warm Aberdeenshire countryside and arrived at Drumblair House, sometime around 6 May 1921. The mansion stands in the little valley of Glen Dronach, near Forgue. Just north of the mansion is Glendronach Distillery, where James Allardes had produced malt whisky since 1826. Williams had just taken on the lease of the mansion house, shootings and hill grazing of Drumblair, and it was his intention to develop them as a sporting estate.

Alighting from his car, Williams stood on the gravel drive in front of his new home. Drumblair was not perhaps one of the grandest of Scottish country houses, but it did at least present some hint of antiquity. The house had originally been erected in the eighteenth century, when it was just a small laird's house of two storeys. In 1877 the previous occupant had decided to try to beef up the appearance of the building, and make it look more like an ancient Scottish castle. However, their funds were limited, and the alterations were little more than a cosmetic exercise. At either end of the main façade little pencil-thin angle turrets were added. Indeed, they were so thin that they were unable to contain any rooms, and simply had blind windows let into the masonry. The tall conical roofs were topped with elaborate thistle-shaped finials.

Roughly central on the main façade a simple square tower was added to create a third storey. This was quite small in plan, and only had one window overlooking the entrance. To add to the appearance of a castle it had a crenellated parapet around the top.

The crenellations were echoed on the small porch below. To architectural eyes Drumblair was a sad mix of traditional Scots vernacular and false baronialism, but to Williams it had all the appearance of a Highland castle, and he was proud to call it his own.

With Colonel Williams came his wife and her son and 18-year-old daughter, Marie. They stood for a short time to take in the grandeur of their new home and then looked down Glen Dronach towards the distillery. The countryside around was part of the parish of Forgue, in the rolling landscape of Strathbogie. A few small hills rose up around them, not particularly high, but sufficiently prominent to given the impression of a glen. To the east was Drumblair Hill, just over 750 feet above sea level. To the north was Boghead Hill, at 620 feet, and to the west were the wooded heights of Frendraught, reaching 740 feet.

Colonel Williams decided that Drumblair required some renovation and redecoration, so he contacted a number of local tradesmen, mainly from Huntly, though some were brought from as far as Aberdeen. Soon various vans were making their way along the drive to the house, where workers found employment replacing pipes, sorting windows, decorating rooms, and supplying all sorts of goods to the new tenants. Food and consumables were also obtained locally, and suppliers brought food, wine, spirits, clothing, guns and other sporting accessories, plate and other goods to Drumblair. In total it was said that 23 or 24 local small merchants and businessmen found their services required.

The renovations were all required for Colonel Williams' new business. He proposed inviting paying guests to the mansion, where he would offer them grouse and rough shooting. He reckoned that he would be able to charge £60 per week from each guest for the shooting, and also 15 shillings and sixpence per day for board and lodging. Williams had numerous old army friends, and many of them had hinted to him that they would be keen to come to his Highland home for sport, should he pursue his idea.

Williams also got himself involved in the local community and was invited to various large house parties in the country, as well as Highland gatherings. He was even invited to perform the opening ceremony at a church sale of work.

Three months after taking on the lease of Drumblair, August 1921 proved to be quite a lucrative month for him. The 'glorious twelfth' of August was the first day of the grouse shooting and Colonel Williams had some of his first guests in residence, ready for the sport. Indeed, throughout the remainder of that month he had a total of 26 guests staying with him, bringing in a tidy income of about £700.

The guests made their way from Drumblair to the moor where they hoped to have a fine week's sport. Local boys were taken on as beaters, and they made their way across the moor to chase birds from the ground and drive them towards the shooters. Spirits were high among the shooters, hoping for a large bag of grouse. Lubricated with whisky prior to the shoot, and sampling more drams from their hip flasks, the shooting party strung itself along the moor to await the birds.

Unfortunately, there were few birds to shoot. Standing around waiting for some grouse to be flushed out, the men began to complain. Eventually the complaints made to Williams were so bad that he agreed that the moor was not particularly good, and that the shooting was poor. He calmed them down by agreeing to lease another moor where the bag would be far better.

Back at Drumblair Williams spent some time trying to find another grouse moor to lease, and soon was able to inform his guests that he had secured the lease of a moor ten miles away. For this he had to pay £250, but at least it calmed the guests and they looked forward to better shooting.

However, it was in August that debtors began to chase Williams for their outstanding accounts to be paid, and the owner of the estate demanded payment of the rent that was now overdue. Williams was unwilling, probably unable, to pay these debts, and soon the police were called in to investigate.

Some of the accounts run up by Williams were being directed to Major-General Sir John Hanbury Williams, KCB, KCVO, CVO, CMG, a distinguished officer in the British army. He was incensed that someone was using either his name, or a name very similar to it, to obtain goods on credit, and that merchants in Aberdeen and district were sending various bills to him for payment, some of which were for significant amounts.

It turned out that Colonel Williams was in fact a bogus laird and, prior to obtaining the lease of Drumblair, he seems to have had no occupation and no fixed home. What was confirmed was that he was born in Highgate, London, in 1867. On 16 August 1911, using the name George Clifford William Wilson, he was appointed Second Lieutenant on probation in the 3rd Battalion of the Shropshire Light Infantry. However, in July 1912 that commission was cancelled. On 3 March 1914 he applied for a commission in the army but his application was refused. A couple of months later, on 15 August 1914, using the name George Williams Wilson, he obtained a commission in the 5th Battalion Middlesex Regiment. He lasted only one year in this regiment, his resignation being requested in October 1915 by the colonel in chief on account of financial difficulties.

Undaunted by his failure in the armed services, Williams applied again for a commission, this time with the Army Veterinary Corps, on 14 May 1916. Using the name George Williams Wilson, he claimed that he had been a captain in the 13th Hussars. His application was checked by the army officials but as they found no record of any service by him in the Hussars his application was turned down.

Williams used his short time in the army to fool others that he had gained rank. In October 1916 he again claimed to have been a captain in the Army Service Corps, commanding Horse

Transport at Winchester. By this time he was using the name Charles Hawfa Williams. Using this identity he was able to obtain various goods on false pretence. His fraud on this occasion was discovered, and he was taken to court. On 16 October 1916 he was convicted at the court of Winchester City Sessions, in Hampshire, of dishonest appropriation of property. He was sentenced to 12 months in prison. On 2 February 1920 a receiving order in bankruptcy was made against Williams and on 8 March 1920 he was adjudged bankrupt. From that time his bankruptcy order had not been discharged.

Undaunted, Williams assumed another nom de plume, that of Lieutenant-Colonel George Hanbury Williams, and claimed that he was the landed proprietor of estates in both England and Wales. These were Hasley Hall, in Warwickshire, and Coldbrook, at Abergavenny in Monmouthshire. He also claimed to be a captain in the 13th Hussars. Using his good name and connections, he wrote to Drumblair's land agent from Boulogne in France on 30 December 1920 and was able to persuade him to give him the lease of the house and moors from May 1921 with a view to purchase. The mansion was the property of Thomas William Robertson, a farmer and landed proprietor, who lived at Birkenhill near Gartly in Aberdeenshire.

With debts mounting, Williams was charged by the police and indicted to appear before the Sheriff at Aberdeen on 5 January 1922. Crowds gathered outside the court to witness the 'Colonel' making his way to the dock. The story had grabbed the attention of the public, and many were there to witness the man whose brazen fraudulency had fooled them all. The cold January weather was hard, and snow fell as they stood for over an hour, hoping to be admitted to the public gallery. A number of policemen were outside the court to keep order, and as soon as the door was opened the crowds rushed in and filled up any public space. Many more people were left outside.

Dressed very much like a country gentleman, Williams arrived at the courthouse shortly after 10 a.m. He walked with a slight stoop, and below a heavy waterproof coat he wore a tweed suit and gamekeeper's cap. Under his arm he carried a bundle wrapped in brown paper. He made his way from the prison van to the back door of the court, handcuffed to a police constable.

The buzz in the courthouse was immense. Proceedings started late, due to the numbers keen to watch. Williams was led into the dock. In the seats immediately to the rear of the dock sat Mrs Williams and their daughter, Marie. The pair chatted nervously to those seated around them. Mrs Williams wore a coney seal fur, and carried a large muff. Marie wore a felt hat, which shaded part of her face. Over a dark-blue loose-hanging dress she wore a heavy coat of a crushed strawberry shade.

The Procurator Fiscal, T. MacLennan, entered the court, closely followed by Sheriff Laing. Representing Williams was Mr Rezin, a solicitor sent north from Birmingham on the instructions of Williams' mother. Eventually, once the court had settled down, the Sheriff Clerk Depute started the proceedings. Sheriff Laing then read out Williams' long list of aliases, before continuing, 'You have been served with the copy of this indictment. Do you plead guilty or not guilty?'

Williams responded, 'Guilty,' speaking in a clear but subdued tone.

On hearing this, the court went silent, but for the rustling of the advocate's papers. In the pause, Williams turned round to look at his wife and daughter. Mrs Williams sat with a steely expression, her face giving away nothing. Marie Williams was less successful in hiding her emotions, for a faint smile crossed her lips as she looked at her father.

Williams turned back and looked at the sheriff. His face was twitching nervously as he gazed forward, and soon he was presented with a pen in order to sign the document before him. He then rose to his feet to await the sheriff's judgment.

George Clifford Charles Williams, alias George Williams Wilson, alias Creswell Charles Claude Herbert Hawfa Williams, alias George Hanbury Williams, in view of the serious nature of the frauds to which you have pleaded guilty, I cannot, consistent with my duty, do other than remit you to the High Court of Justiciary for sentence.

The crowd in the court murmured quietly amongst themselves. This was not what they had expected. They thought that the sentence would be handed out in Aberdeen and that Williams would have to serve his time locally.

Looking neither to one side nor the other, Williams stood down from the dock. He produced a tweed hat from his jacket, which he wore low down over his face as he was escorted out of the court. In the rear precincts of the building, Williams was temporarily reunited with his family. Mrs Williams had sent him a note, after which a policeman escorted her and Marie to the room where Williams was held. They were allowed ten minutes alone together, during which time Williams hugged his wife and gently kissed his daughter. He was then led off to spend the next few days in Craiginches Prison in Aberdeen.

At the High Court in Edinburgh on Monday 16 January 1922, Williams appeared before the Lord Justice General. Prosecuting for the Crown were the Lord Advocate, Mr T.B. Morrison, KC, MP, and the advocate depute, Mr Fenton. Williams wore a heavy brown waterproof coat. Again the court was crowded, the case having elicited much interest. To defend him was Mr Sam MacDonald, advocate.

Williams was charged with having invented a fraudulent scheme whereby he obtained a long lease of the mansion house and shootings of Drumblair. To get these he had claimed to be George Hanbury Williams, a lieutenant-colonel in the British Army. As collateral to guarantee his rent he claimed that he was the owner of two estates in England, as well as one in Ireland. It was claimed by him that the English estates brought in an income of around £3,000 per annum.

Another of Williams' claims was that he had married for a second time, and that his current wife was Lady Mercer, a relation of the Duke of Sutherland. To prove his connections in high places, Williams claimed that he was related to the Duke of Richmond and Gordon. Indeed, he claimed that a great aunt of the Duke's was in fact his own grandmother.

Using these connections and false claims of income from English estates, Williams was able to take on the lease of Drumblair, both house and shootings, for a period of ten years, paying £350 per annum. He also acquired the hill grazing of the estate for a further £75 per annum. Taking possession at the beginning of May, he was due to pay the first instalment of rent on 1 August that year. However, the date passed and he made no payment to the owner.

Williams was also charged that he had taken on the services of almost two dozen local tradesmen and suppliers, without intending to pay them. In total it was reckoned that he owed them around £323.

The police had been searching through Williams' past, and discovered that this was not the first financial fraud that he had been charged with. It was also discovered that his wife was the widow of a joiner from Clitheroe, Lancashire, and that she and Williams were married in 1911.

Sam MacDonald claimed that Williams had taken on the lease with good intentions, and that it had been his plan to make the estate and shootings a money-making scheme. He had apparently been persuaded by many of his old army friends that he should take an estate in Scotland with shooting and fishing, and that they would come and pay to take part in the shooting. Whilst there, they would pay for their lodgings within the mansion.

The defence informed the court that during the month of August Williams had taken in 26 guests. When the guests complained that the shooting was not of a suitable standard, Williams had leased another grouse moor for which he had to pay £250. This money had been paid to the owner of the moor, which was used in his defence as indicative of his willingness to pay to try to make the business a success.

Other expenses Williams had paid out included the first instalment in the hire purchase of a car, which cost £86. He had also paid around £800 to various tradesmen for work at the mansion house. However, with his guests leaving due to the poor shooting, he was left with little income and no chance of paying off his debts. Mr MacDonald, in Williams' defence, asked the court to be lenient with him, explaining that he should have been up before the Bankruptcy Court instead of the High Court, and that he was only here due to his colourful claims of connections in high places which he used to obtain the lease of Drumblair.

Williams pleaded guilty to the charges, and the Lord Justice General summed up:

> The charges to which you have pleaded guilty are not charges of having undertaken an unsuccessful commercial speculation. They are charges of fraud. They disclose an extensive course of fraud which, under whatever circumstances it was entered upon, cannot have been prosecuted otherwise than with deliberation, and certainly with unusual callous persistency. Conduct of that kind strikes at the root of the credit and mutual confidence without which society would go to pieces. It was conduct, moreover, that is heinous to the law. I bear in mind all that your counsel has said on your behalf, but I feel I cannot do my duty if I impose on you a sentence less than the one which I now pass of five years' penal servitude.

Williams listened intently as the Lord Justice General addressed him. It was noted that when he heard that he was to be locked up for five years he made no indication of surprise. He was then led away to begin his term in gaol.

On Friday 29 December Williams' wife left Drumblair and moved south to England. She stated that their trouble was due to her husband's big ideas. Wishing to begin life afresh, she had suggested to him that they run a small hotel; but he would have nothing less than a shooting lodge. She informed an interviewer that they had done well during their first month at Drumblair, bringing in no less than £600 from paying guests.

# 14

## 'Antique' Smith: Alexander Howland Smith

The *Cumnock Express*, a now-defunct newspaper that served the small Ayrshire town of that name, published an article in August 1892 concerning a letter that had turned up, apparently written by Robert Burns, Scotland's great poet. The letter had been written by the bard to 'Mr John Hill, weaver, Cumnock', and had been published by the paper for its local interest.

One of the readers of the newspaper, W. Craibe Angus of Glasgow, spotted the article, and as he was a keen Burnsian and something of a local historian, he decided to do some investigating. He then wrote to the newspaper claiming that the letter was very unlike Burns' others letters and, on further investigation, no evidence of a John Hill in Cumnock could be found.

James MacKenzie, of 2 Rillbank Crescent, just off the East Meadows, Edinburgh, who had sent the letter to the *Cumnock Express*, was incensed at the insinuation that he was the owner of a forgery, and that he was unable to decide whether the letter was genuine or not. He was a keen collector of antiques, and was also a Fellow of the Society of Antiquaries of Scotland. He was a chemist by trade, and he reckoned that he was competent enough to decide whether or not the letter was real. He wrote to the Cumnock paper arguing against Angus (who had written anonymously), dismissing his thoughts as being incompetent and worthless. In his letter he claimed that the Burns document had been 'attested fully by those who are thoroughly competent to judge'.

Angus was quick to reply, and revealed himself in his next letter. He demanded that MacKenzie should reveal who the competent judges were, and stated that only the decisions of experts at the British Museum would be good enough to satisfy him. Others began to take an interest in the dispute, and H.D. Colvill-Scott of Surrey, who was a noted collector of Burns' manuscripts of the time, came down on the side of Angus, agreeing that the letter was bogus.

MacKenzie was still adamant that he was right, and sent off another letter to the newspaper, appending a copy of yet another undiscovered Burns manuscript, which contained the poem 'To the Rosebud'. This failed to convince Angus and Colvill-Scott, and MacKenzie sent off yet another poem, which he claimed had been 'written by Burns after hearing a sermon preached in Tarbolton Church'.

MacKenzie, amazingly, was able to produce yet another Burns poem, entitled 'The Poor Man's Prayer'. This was to go far in bringing about his spectacular downfall, for it was discovered to have been published in *The London Magazine* in 1766. In the journal the poem was ascribed to Simon Hedge, a labourer, which was in fact the pen-name of William Hayward Roberts, who was later to become Provost of Eton. The poem, which refers to the homely wishes of the poor man, makes reference to his pleasures of being at home with his children, hardly the sentiments likely to have been thought of by a seven-year-old, as Burns would have been at the time. Indeed, Burns records in his own writings that he 'first committed the sin of rhyme' in honour of 'Handsome Nell', sometime in the autumn of 1774, at the age of 15.

In May 1891 James MacKenzie decided to sell his 'Rillbank Crescent Collection' of ancient documents, which he had been compiling for 25 years. Perhaps he had an inkling, or knew that they were forgeries. When challenged regarding the Tarbolton and 'Poor Man' poems he became very flustered and claimed that he had discovered them in a secret drawer in an old item of furniture he had acquired. At the sale the auctioneer announced to the crowd that some people had claimed that the lot before him were forgeries, but he had looked at them and thought they were genuine. He would not be able to offer any guarantee. The doubt placed in the crowd's mind resulted in it being knocked down for a low figure. Five letters by Burns with his signature and one poem went for less than 2 guineas. A song by the poet went for 30 shillings.

The furore over the letters and poems caused something of an uproar that year, and the whole situation was further inflamed when an Edinburgh bookseller was cited in court as having supplied a rich New York banker, John Stewart Kennedy, with hundreds of literary fakes. The seller of ancient manuscripts and documents was James Stillie, an octogenarian, who had been selling books and letters in his 'Old Book Establishment' at 19 George Street, Edinburgh, for over 50 years. It also turned out that Stillie was the person whom MacKenzie claimed was 'competent to judge'. In his youth Stillie had worked for John Ballantyne & Company, booksellers and auctioneers, one of the directors of which was Sir Walter Scott. Scott often sent his scrapbooks there for binding, and the young Stillie took a great interest in them.

With the growing furore into the forgeries, James Stillie took out a double-page advertisement in the first issue of the *Burns Chronicle* of 1891. In it he recorded:

I have been sadly annoyed with certain self-elected Experts and Pretenders regarding Burns Manuscripts, in the West of Scotland, chiefly in Glasgow, one hitherto respectable firm wrote me a particular account of Forgeries of Burns in Edinburgh. I immediately challenged them for their Authority and required the name but they giving me no Authority I wrote them that the statement was quite untrue, and a malicious scandal on Edinburgh.

In Edinburgh at the time a document with Burns' signature on it could have sold for around 30 shillings.

Kennedy had been buying letters and original writings from Stillie for a number of years, being an avid collector of such material. Many of them he donated to museums and libraries across America, and he was hailed as a great benefactor in the country. Doubts arose over the origins of some of these documents, and Kennedy took Stillie to court. The British Museum was given the task of checking Kennedy's collection, and of 202 manuscripts purchased by him from Stillie, only one turned out to be genuine, and it was the one previously regarded as the least important of the entire collection. Kennedy took Stillie to court, in an attempt to recover the £750 he had spent on the collection. The civil case was heard in Edinburgh, where Stillie denied that he sold the documents as genuine, and also that they were forged. As the case went on he eventually claimed that he was now 87 and so was unsure of what he was doing. His sorry appearance and manner was such that Kennedy was persuaded to drop the case.

However, the forgeries had been discovered, and further investigation continued. The Kennedy collection, which included papers written by people such as John Graham of Claverhouse, Rob Roy MacGregor and Mary, Queen of Scots was discovered to have been almost entirely written on the same type of paper with a similar ink, despite the many years separating the supposed dates of origin.

The *Edinburgh Evening Dispatch*, under the editorship of William Riach, took the investigative torch from the *Cumnock Express*, and ran even faster and further with it. They enquired around the sale rooms and antique book dealers of Edinburgh, and discovered that many of the forged documents had passed through the hands of Andrew Brown, a bookseller at 15 Bristo Place, just beyond the southern end of George IV Bridge. 'Bristo' Brown, as he was known, was found to have sold many of the manuscripts on, and appeared to be a middleman. Previously, in 1886, he had tried to sell an album containing letters and autographs from famous writers such as James Hogg, Sir Walter Scott and William Makepeace Thackeray. One interested client refused to buy, reckoning that the album was priced too cheaply if it was genuine, and because many of the letters by different authors, as well as the pencilled descriptions of each on the album pages, were too alike. However, 'Bristo' Brown bought it from Smith for 15 shillings and sold it on shortly afterwards for £1.

The album had in fact been offered to Brown by Alexander Howland Smith. He worked as chief clerk in the office of Thomas Henry Ferrier, Writer to the Signet. Ferrier's father had been an agent to a number of important people, and as a result had hundreds of letters from them stored in the office. Smith claimed that Ferrier told him to tidy up the office at one time, and that he could throw out many of the old and seemingly useless documents. Smith claimed that he thought some of them interesting, so took them home to read. It was during this time that he claimed to have discovered the old letters and autographs which he later sold. One of these was claimed to have been an original poem by Robert Burns. When 'Bristo' Brown checked with Thomas Ferrier whether Smith was telling the truth, and whether he had any right to the letters, he replied that it was certainly possible.

'Bristo' Brown bought many more documents from Smith and did not even question Smith when, despite the fact that he was dismissed by Ferrier in June 1885, the letters kept on coming. Smith had been accused of stealing two cheques belonging to the firm and had been charged by the police. When the case went to court Smith was found innocent of the crime, yet Ferrier still paid him off.

In its quest to track down the forger, the *Evening Dispatch* reported on 22 November 1892, 'There has been of late years, we are assured, a most systematic and wholesale forgery of letters purporting to be written by Scott and Burns.' In later issues the paper explained how to detect forgeries and by December it had compiled a list of hundreds of forgeries that had turned up. These included no fewer than 130 works by Robert Burns, as well as papers by Bonnie Prince Charlie, Oliver Cromwell, Scott, Thackeray, and many others.

Some of the manuscripts were offered to museums, but in most cases they were able to spot that they were fraudulent. The Carnegie Library in Ayr was offered an original manuscript by Burns entitled 'The Bonnie Banks of Ayr' by someone who had purchased it. The library was delighted with the manuscript but later discovered that it was a fake. Similarly the Burns Monument and Museum in Kilmarnock had been offered various manuscripts in November 1892 that they were able to identify as fake.

Word spread to other newspapers of forged manuscripts coming from a 'factory' in Edinburgh. *The Daily Telegraph* reported that 'punishment sufficiently severe for the Scotsman who would forge letters and poems by Scott and Burns in order to beguile the inexperienced collector could hardly be either imagined or invented. Hurling him from the top of the Castle Rock at Edinburgh would be far too mild for the offence.'

The *Evening Dispatch* kept up the search, and in one issue published a copy of one of the forgeries. A *Dispatch* reader, a Mr Ferrier, recognised the handwriting and informed the paper that it belonged to a clerk who used to work for him. The reader was even able to supply an original letter by the clerk, so that the handwriting could be compared. The *Dispatch* traced the forger, and was able to give a detailed description of the man:

The person of whose calligraphy we have given specimens is A.H. Smith who occupies lodgings in Brunswick Street . . . He appears to be a little over thirty years of age, of sallow complexion, with dark moustache and slight side whiskers. The expression of his countenance is unanimated; rather he looks dull, and appears mildly mannered. He has a plausible, insinuating way with him, although he would be the last person whose appearance should lead one to suspect him guilty of such a mass of manuscripts . . . Among his friends he is known as 'Antique' Smith, from frequently having with him old documents or curiosities of various kinds for sale.

The quest had tracked down Alexander Smith, a bachelor, born in 1859, who lived at 87 Brunswick Street. He also had a small summer house located in the allotments at Hopetoun Crescent, on the opposite side of Leith Walk from his lodgings. It was in this small building that he produced his many forgeries. He also stored many other antiquities here, acquiring them and doing them up before selling them on to antique dealers. He is also reported as having dealt to some extent in paintings, though it is not known whether he actually painted them or passed on works by others.

When approached by the *Dispatch*, Smith denied that he was the source of the forgeries, claiming that there was nothing to connect him with them. However, further investigations by the paper discovered that he had been a regular seller to local antique dealers, and that they had purchased many manuscripts from him.

Smith often visited old bookshops, purchasing numerous volumes. It had been noted with hindsight by many of the dealers that he was quite strange in his selection, often taking books in large quantities, yet not keeping to any obvious subject or pattern. The pattern was in fact quite fixed – he bought books that had blank pages within them, to give him old paper on which to forge his letters. It was also noted that Smith preferred to take his purchases with him, and refused to allow delivery, so that the dealers could never discover who he was, or where he lived.

The forgeries produced, Smith then had to sell them on. He employed a number of methods to do this. One of his more common ways was to engage in conversation with other collectors and sell directly to them. Another was to send the manuscripts to auction houses for sale. Sometimes he visited Edinburgh pawn shops and offered them manuscripts in return for a loan. This was probably the method he employed when a forgery was not up to his usual high standard and would perhaps have been spotted as fake by a good antiques dealer. Smith would then fail to redeem his pawn, and the brokers would send the manuscripts to the auction rooms themselves, to recoup their money.

Smith produced forged manuscripts by many different people. He turned out works by Robert Burns, Mary Queen of Scots, Lord Darnley, the Earl of Bothwell, various Stuart kings, Oliver Cromwell, the Marquis of Montrose, Bonnie Prince Charlie, Flora MacDonald, James Hogg, the Duke of Wellington, Lord Nelson, Sir Walter Scott, Lord Byron, William Thackeray, Thomas Carlyle, and almost anyone else to order.

By now the police were involved, and at around 7.30 p.m. on 5 December 1892 Smith was arrested in the capital's Rose Street. He was taken to gaol and later appeared at the Burgh Court, charged with 'selling and pawning spurious MSS as genuine, obtaining money by pretending that certain documents were genuine and what they purported to be, and by certain false stories as to their origin, you knowing the said documents to be false'. He was informed that he was not charged with forgery, for it was not a crime to produce false documents. It was a crime to obtain money claiming that the items were genuine. Smith applied for bail but at first this was refused. He applied again a few days later, and this time he was released on payment of a surety of £100. Smith then went to court himself and was successful in receiving an order preventing the *Dispatch* from printing any further articles about him.

The trial did not take place until 25 June 1893. Held at the High Court of Justiciary in Edinburgh, it lasted over two days. At the court 162 different forged documents were produced as evidence, along with a book that belonged to Smith, *The Autographic Mirror*, which explained how to copy letters. It was expected that the prosecution would call 47 witnesses.

The documents were sent to expert chemists who studied them closely. At first they came back with the claim that the forgeries were very cleverly done, and that it had been difficult to prove that they were not genuine. But later it transpired that the chemists were able to state with conviction that the letters had all been written with the same ink, despite their having been written by different people over a 150-year period!

George Frederick Warner, assistant keeper of manuscripts at the British Museum, was also called upon to examine the paper used in the letters. He could prove that some of the paper had been taken from books, and that some sheets had been created by a more modern method of paper-making than was current at the time when they were supposed to have been written. Many of them had been tinged with tea stains or other colouring agents, to add further antique effect. Warner also stated in court that the letters all appeared to have been written by a single hand.

Other experts who had studied the supposed writers or recipients of the letters could point out numerous errors of factual content within them. Although Smith had done a reasonable amount of research into the writers of the letters, he did not know enough to make sure that what he was writing about could have in fact taken place. One of the documents was supposed to have been signed by Burns in 1793, but the signature had been written with a steel-nibbed pen, something that Burns did not own. Another document was supposed to be been Rev. Richard Cameron's dying declaration, prior to being executed in

Edinburgh. In fact, the Covenanter leader had been killed at the Battle of Airds Moss in Ayrshire on 22 June 1680. Another document had John Graham of Claverhouse signing his name a few days after he had been killed on the battlefield of Killiekrankie.

Two letters were produced that were written by different people and were sent to different correspondents, but both letters contained the exact same words. A poem by Robert Burns turned out to be a verse by Alexander Pope.

A letter with some verses by Lord Byron was discovered to have been written on modern paper, and the handwriting was rather rough, indicative of someone copying the style, rather than fluently writing as they would have. In addition, this letter was folded in a manner that would imply it was to be put into an envelope, something that did not exist in Byron's times.

The Edinburgh bookseller, George Thin, who had a bookshop on South Bridge, had purchased two of Smith's forgeries in the spring of 1890 for £12. These he had acquired at a sale of items pawned with the Equitable Loan Company but which had never been redeemed. Thin did not regard the letters as frauds when he saw them in the dim light of the saleroom, but when he returned to his office and studied them he had doubts over their authenticity.

Smith's defence was extremely poor. The best he could come up with were testimonies from his sister, Agnes Smith, and a lodger who used to live with him, both of whom could confirm that they had never seen him forge any documents. Agnes stated that on one occasion she had gone to her brother's work at Ferrier's office. Whilst there he had shown her into a vault in which there were hundreds of ancient documents and deed boxes, some of which he had at home. Another attempt at defending Smith was abandoned when they realised that blaming 'Bristo' Brown, who 'must' have known that the letters were forged, implied that Smith was in fact guilty of producing them!

The defence then tried to claim that there had been no crime committed as those who had purchased the documents had not lost any money in doing so, and in fact had made a profit when they sold them on. However, the Lord Justice Clerk pointed out that the crime was 'fabricating and disposing of historical and literary manuscripts', and that what happened to them afterwards was nothing to do with the case currently under consideration.

There was little made of the fact that Smith claimed that he had been given the right to sell on some of the old documents from Ferrier's vaults. On one occasion, when he was asked by George Tait, of the Equitable Loan Company, if he had the right to remove such documents from Ferrier's office, he produced a handwritten will in which Thomas Ferrier wrote, 'I hereby bequeath to my nephew Alexander Smith, the whole of my valuable MSS.' This will was, of course, a fake itself.

Once the jury went out to consider its verdict, they came to a conclusion very quickly, only taking half an hour. Smith was found guilty, but the jury recommended that he should be treated with leniency. They reckoned that the crime had caused no great harm to anyone, and that the dealers in forged documents had been guilty to some extent of pushing for more manuscripts. The Lord Justice Clerk summed up:

> Alexander Howland Smith, the crime of which you have been convicted is a serious one, particularly in the view that you evidently were following the course of concocting documents in order practically to make a livelihood by selling them. I am giving all the effect I can to the recommendation of the jury in abstaining from pronouncing a sentence of penal servitude, and sentencing you to imprisonment for twelve calendar months.

Smith served his time in Calton Gaol, Edinburgh, but it was never known just how much of his work had passed into the hands of collectors undetected. Many of the documents were handed over to the National Library of Scotland, which had them stamped with the word 'Spurious'. In the national collection there are many of Smith's originals, which themselves have now earned a degree of interest.

One of Smith's manuscripts turned up at Christie's auction room in Glasgow on 23 June 1976, where it was offered for sale as the original Burns letter to John Buego, engraver of many illustrations that appeared in some versions of his poems. It was written from Ellisland on 9 September 1788. However, Burns experts knew that the original letter was in fact in the National Museum of Antiquities in Edinburgh. As the Museum of Antiquities was not selling the original, the letter offered at Christie's must have been a forgery. It was withdrawn from the sale and it is reckoned that it was probably an 'Antique' Smith copy.

As recently as 1977, the Burns Monument Trustees in Alloway, Ayrshire, purchased a number of supposed letters, poems and songs by Robert Burns that were known to have been forged. These were bought for their curio value. Comprising 11 songs, eight poems and three letters, the forgeries purchased by the Monument trustees had been written in brown ink, which was unlike that used by Burns. They had also been endorsed by a publisher, but the ink used by the publisher and style of writing appeared to have been the same as Burns' own!

On his release from gaol, Smith was able to set himself up in business, buying and selling old manuscripts, curios, antiques and books. His premises were at 26 George Street, but it is not known whether all his deals were done on the straight and narrow thereafter. It is not known when Smith died, but the last-known letter from Smith, to a fellow bookseller in Edinburgh, James Cameron of St David Street, is dated 20 November 1905.

# 15
# Electric Medicine:
# 'Doctor' James Graham

There was great excitement when Doctor James Graham's new establishment opened for business in August 1779. Situated in London's fashionable St James's, at 81 Pall Mall, the 'Temple Æsculapio Sacrum', or the Temple of Health, had cost him over £10,000 to create, and the upper classes of the capital waited on its opening with keen anticipation. The admission fee was two shillings and sixpence, for which the client received entry to the temple. Further services would cost him more – a tour of the whole temple and participation in the full essence of Elysian sensuality cost ten shillings and sixpence.

Prior to the gala opening, Graham had hired two massive men who were nicknamed 'Gog' and 'Magog', from Revelation 20:8, where they represent the two nations at the Apocalypse. They were dressed in gold-trimmed uniforms and were paid to wander through the streets of London, giving out handbills inscribed:

The Temple of Health:
The Magnificent Electrical Apparatus and the supremely brilliant and unique decorations of this magical edifice – of this enchanting Elysian Palace! Where wit and mirth, love and beauty – all that can

150

delight the soul and all that can ravish the senses, will hold their court, this and every evening this week, in chaste and joyous assemblage. The Celestial brilliance of the Medico-Electrical Apparatus in all the apartments of the temple will be exhibited by Dr Graham himself, who will have the honour of explaining the true nature and effects of electricity, air, music, and magnetism, when applied to the human body.

Precisely at eight o'clock the Gentleman Usher of the Rosy Rod, assisted by the High Priestess, will conduct the rosy, the gigantic, the STUPENDOUS Goddess of Health to the Celestial Throne. The blooming Priestess of the Temple will endeavour to entertain Ladies and Gentlemen of candour and good nature, by reading a lecture on the simplest and most efficacious means of preserving health, beauty, and personal loveliness, and a serene mental brilliancy even to the extremest old age. Vestina the Gigantic, on the Celestial Throne, as the Goddess of Health, will exhibit in her own person a proof of the all-blessing effects of virtue, temperance, regularity, simplicity, and moderation; and in these luxurious, artificial and effeminate times, to recommend those great virtues.

Inside this magnificently decorated house the patients could walk around the richly furnished corridors and visit the various rooms. Each was decorated to the highest standard, and the furnishings were of the latest design. In addition, wafts of the finest perfume made their way through the apartments, and the sound of music permeated the building.

One room in the Temple had a number of chairs within it, where visitors could sit and listen to Graham delivering one of his many lectures. These were usually on health topics, but Graham had developed his public speaking skills and the talks were very entertaining. Graham was noted as a showman, and his appearance was handsome.

Within another room there was a variety of medicines on sale, many of which were unavailable at any other doctor's practice. Ether was one of the main drugs available, a phial of Electrical Ether being sold for use in preventing germs from the city affecting the patient. Graham advised that the ether should be sniffed whilst in crowded locations, such as the theatre, in court buildings or churches. 'Imperial Pills' were offered for the purification of the blood. These were supposed to cleanse the body of the germs and dirt of the city, and could also increase the client's sex drive. Another wonder cure was Nervous Etherial Balsam, used for treating those who were suffering from a type of depression. It was claimed that the balsam helped to calm nerves, but a useful side effect was its aphrodisiacal qualities, and thus it was in demand by young couples. Graham's 'Elixir of Life' contained nutrients that he claimed would prolong the patient's life, often advertised as 'indefinitely'.

The various cures on sale were available at a variety of prices, designed to suit the pocket of the customer. They were on sale in different quantities at either five shillings per box or bottle, ten shillings and sixpence, or a guinea. Bulk loads were available as well and, if the customer required it, a five-guinea order could be supplied in polished mahogany boxes. Larger quantities were also available.

Another apartment had a number of special medical instruments on display, unique 'medico-electrical' apparatus, which had been brought from his previous practice, and which had apparently originated in the United States.

Although these medical wonders attracted many nosey clients, there were some other things on show that would encourage them to return, often on a regular basis. Walking around the rooms, supposedly in the background, were a number of women, dressed in gossamer-fine silks, draped over their nubile young bodies. They stood in alcoves and corners, lost among the alabaster statues, striking poses like Greek goddesses.

In one of the main rooms of the Temple of Health was a large and ornate bed. Bigger than usual beds, it measured 12 feet in length and was 9 feet wide. The base could be angled to suit the client's preference. It was finely carved, with ornately gilded legs, a sumptuously upholstered headboard and a soft downy mattress. This comprised fresh straw from wheat or oat fields, through which were rose petals, lavender flowers and balm, as well as hair from the tails of stallions. Known as the 'Celestial Bed', customers had to pay £50 per night to sleep in it. Graham claimed that any couples who spent the night in this bed would be 'blessed with progeny'.

During the evening, as the lovers lay in the bed, soft music was played by musicians nearby, and scented candles and essence percolated the air. Above the headboard was a special device that created electrical sparks which filled the room with a so-called magnetic fluid, which was 'calculated to give the necessary degree of strength and exertion to the nerves'. On the ceiling above the bed was suspended a glass mirror, so that the lovers could look up at each other as they lay together. Graham himself claimed that 'the barren must certainly become more fruitful when they are powerfully agitated in the delights of love'. His advertisement gives a detailed indication of what awaited the amorous couple:

> The super-celestial dome of the bed, which contains the odoriferous, balmy and ethereal spices, odours and essences, which is the grand reservoir of those reviving invigorating influences which are exhaled by the breath of the music and by the exhilarating force of electrical fire, is covered on the other side with brilliant panes of looking-glass. On the utmost summit of the dome are placed two exquisite figures of Cupid and Psyche, with a figure of Hymen behind, with his torch flaming with electrical fire in one hand and with the other, supporting a celestial crown, sparkling over a pair of living turtle doves, on a little bed of roses. The other elegant group of figures which sport on the top of the dome, having each of them musical instruments in their hands,

which by the most expensive mechanism, breathe forth sound corresponding to their instruments, flutes, guitars, violins, clarinets, trumpets, horns, oboes, kettle drums, etc. The post, or pillars, too, which support the grand dome, are groups of musical instruments, golden pipes, etc., which in sweet concert breathe forth celestial sounds, lulling the visions of Elysian joys. At the head of the bed appears sparkling with electrical fire a great first commandment: BE FRUITFUL, MULTIPLY AND REPLENISH THE EARTH. Under that is an elegant sweet-toned organ in front of which is a fine landscape of moving figures, priest and bride's procession entering the Temple of Hymen. In the Celestial Bed no feather bed is employed but sometimes mattresses filled with sweet new wheat or oat straw mingled with balm, rose leaves, lavender flowers and oriental spices. The sheets are of the richest and softest silk, stained colour, sky blue, white and purple, and are sweetly perfumed in oriental manner with the Tudor rose, or with rich gums or balsams. The chief principle of my Celestial Bed is produced by artificial lodestones. About 15 cwt. of compound magnets are continually pouring forth in an ever flowing circle. The bed is constructed with a double frame, which moves on an axis or pivot and can be converted into an inclined plane. Sometimes the mattresses are filled with the strongest, most springy hair, produced at vast expense from the tails of English stallions which are elastic to the highest degree.

Advertised as a cure for sterility or impotence, the bedroom was in fact probably little more than a front for an upmarket brothel. It even had its own private entrance from the street. The whole Temple was built on sex, though styled more on the classical Greek or Roman lines, with voluptuous maidens wandering around, attending to the needs of the clientele.

James Graham was born in Edinburgh's Grassmarket (although some accounts state that he was born in the capital's Cowgate, which is a continuation of the same street) in 1745, the son of a saddler. He was educated in the city, and his father had sufficient funds to allow him to study medicine at the University of Edinburgh. Graham never qualified, failing to complete his studies for one reason or another. Despite this, he set himself up as a medical practitioner, and whether it was his clients who started referring to him as a doctor, or whether he promoted the use of this title himself, he soon became known as Doctor Graham.

Around 1770 James Graham emigrated to America. At first he travelled around the country, spending some time in New England, but he eventually settled in Philadelphia. There he set himself up in a practice where he claimed to be a specialist in the treatment of eyes.

At the time Graham was in North America Dr Benjamin Franklin was conducting experiments in the use of electricity. Franklin (1706–90) had discovered that there were positive and negative charges of electricity and the new discoveries were the talk of the press at the time. Graham became deeply interested in this, and he thought that electricity was to become a major new method for treating various ailments, something of a panacea for all ills. He noted that 'electricity invigorates the whole body and remedies all physical defects'. Graham was one of a number who believed that 'electric medicine' could be used to treat almost anything.

In 1775 Graham moved back to Britain. He appears to have opened up medical consulting rooms in Bath and Bristol, but within a short period of time moved and settled in London. He opened a small practice where he introduced the electric methods of treating patients, convinced that he could make his fortune with it. His patients were mainly from the rich and famous classes, and his reputation as a successful doctor resulted in a large following. The methods used by him varied, one of the 'cures' being to give the patient a fair-sized electric shock using a variety of prods and crowns.

One of Graham's first patients was none other than Catherine Macaulay (1731–91), a notable British historian of the time. She was to sign a number of testimonials that were used to advertise Graham's business and introduce more customers to his practice. Macaulay was later to marry Graham's younger brother, William. With Macaulay's influential connections, soon James Graham became a doctor who attracted the aristocracy.

One of those who frequently used Graham's services was Georgiana (1757–1806), wife of the 5th Duke of Devonshire. She was greatly impressed by Graham's various treatments, and was influential in persuading others to attend. A fashionable beauty of the time, she is noted for canvassing for Charles James Fox in the Westminster elections by giving kisses in return for a promise to vote for him.

Within his medical practice, Graham supplied 'aetherial balsams' for the patients. They were then invited to sit on his 'magnetic throne', the magnetism supplied by the use of lodestone. Other patients may have been invited to bathe in electrical baths. Although some patients were to claim that Graham was little more than a 'quack', his treatments appealed to many customers, and he was always introducing the latest 'discoveries' and most up-to-date equipment.

The success of his electrical medical practice was not enough for Graham. He decided to open his Temple of Health, and acquired a large Georgian town house in one of the better districts of London. When it was opened, the Temple of Health attracted a large number of customers. The building used by Graham is known as Schomberg House, parts of which were erected in 1694 by the Countess of Portland. A four-storey building, it is quite an unusual style for London, and is constructed of red brick. Prior to Graham taking it on, it was the property of John Astley (1724–87), an artist who created a studio on the roof. His neighbour at number 82, during the time of the Temple, was the famous portrait painter, Thomas Gainsborough. Today the façade of Schomberg House has been retained, but a modern office block of 1956 sits behind it.

Patrons of the Temple would enter by the front door, passing the liveried porters, Gog and Magog, their size emphasized by their uniforms and tri-cornered hats. Although presented as porters, the two men were also bouncers, able to remove any unsuitable clients. Within the entrance hall was a statue of Æsculapius, the 'father of healing'. Here the client paid their admission fee, before continuing along the main corridor. Strategically placed along this were a variety of crutches, spectacles, slings and splints, supposedly left behind by those cured on previous visits. The patient then entered a main apartment, sumptuously furnished.

At first glance this room was fitted out in the style of a Greek temple. But closer inspection revealed that the statues, paintings and stained-glass windows had a sex-based theme, all designed to get the patient aroused. Candles burned in holders, the scented wax giving off a richly perfumed aroma that filled the space.

On the first floor of the building the rooms contained a different style of furnishing. They were filled with electrical apparatus, which Graham claimed would cure a wide variety of ailments. Many of them could produce sparks of electricity, or 'celestial fire' as he termed it, which in most cases were passed through the body to bring healing. There were also a variety of other pseudo-medical items, such as large bottles and test tubes filled with different chemicals and perfumes, some of them bubbling to give off a scent, others attracting the wondering gazes of the clientele due to their bright colours.

Doctor Graham's lectures were usually on the subject of human health, but most of these bordered on the lewd, and were probably only designed to titillate. Within some rooms were 'Goddesses of Youth and Health', who also delivered talks on a variety of subjects associated with beauty and lovemaking. That they were little more than upmarket peepshows was evident by the fact that they only wore silken robes, and on many occasions appeared in a near-naked state. These 'warm lectures' were written by Graham himself, and were his thoughts on what love was, and how couples could achieve it.

Graham's entourage of attractive young women is thought to have included one young lady who was later to make her mark on history in a different way. Emma (or Amy) Lyon is said to have been one of the scantily clad goddesses who worked in the Temple. As with most of the girls who worked there, she was recruited through advertisements in the local newspapers. Only 16 at the time she was employed by Graham, she went by the name of 'Hebe Vestina' in the Temple. At first it is thought that she was a singer in the building, but she later became one of the main attractions, the goddess 'Hygiea', cavorting scantily in the thinnest of robes. In another of her performances she cavorted around naked in a mud bath. Emma Lyon later left the Temple and became a lady renowned for playing around. She married Sir William Hamilton, thus becoming Lady Emma, and was to find lasting notoriety as the mistress of Lord Horatio Nelson.

Others known to have visited Graham's sexual Temple include the politician Charles James Fox (1749–1806), the Prince of Wales (later King George IV), and Mary Darby, or Mrs Robinson (1758–1800), who was the Prince of Wales' mistress.

Not every customer who passed through the Temple of Health was delighted with what he saw or experienced. Horace Walpole visited the building and recorded his thoughts in his journal:

It is the most impudent puppet-show of imposition I ever saw, and the mountebank himself is the dullest of his profession. A woman, invisible, warbled to clarinets on the stairs. The decorations are pretty and odd, and the apothecary, who comes up a trap-door (for no purpose, since he might as well come up the stairs), is a novelty. The electrical experiments are nothing at all singular, and a poor air-pump, that only bursts a bladder, pieces out the farce.

Although overall the Temple of Health was initially a resounding success, it failed to make Graham a fortune. Basically operated as a high-class brothel and gambling den, the Temple was raided a number of times by the police. A London cartoonist published an image of Graham and another sexual therapist, the German Mr Katterfella, in 1783. They are standing facing each other, as though in battle, with large phallic objects aimed at each other. Doctor Graham speaks in a speech bubble, 'That round Vigour! That full toned juvenile virility which speaks so cordially and so effectually home to the Female heart, conciliating its Favours & Friendship, and riveting its Interest Affections. Away thou German Maggot killer, thy fame is not to be Compar'd to mine.' Graham straddles the 'Prime Conductor, Gentle Restorer' glass tube, which is noticed as being the 'Largest in the World' and insulated, indicating its electric charge. Looking on are Gog and Magog, and supporting Graham in this competition is a duck, indicative that he is a Scottish Quack, emphasised by the thistle in the duck's 'quack bubble'.

In 1782 Graham was so much in debt that he had to sell up and he moved back to Edinburgh the following year. By this time he had decided that electric medicine was not all it was cracked up to be, and that instead mud baths were the future. He opened a new establishment in the city where large baths filled with a variety of muds were located.

Graham claimed that bathing in mud would result in immortality. Instead of eating, Graham claimed that users of his baths would absorb all the nutrients that their bodies required in order to live, thus helping the patient to lose weight and gain health. Graham himself claimed to have spent two weeks in a bath full of mud, eating nothing and taking only a few small sips of water.

Graham also continued with his lectures, one of these being entitled, 'On the Means of exciting and rendering permanent the rational, temperate and serene pleasures of the married state.' This shocked the sober citizens of Edinburgh and the authorities banned him from giving lectures, due to the 'coarseness and indecency' of their content.

Nevertheless, sales of his book, *The Guardian of Health, Happiness and Long Life*, was in demand for its titillating content, copies being sold direct to purchasers wrapped in a plain brown cover. Another of Graham's treatises, *Private Advisers*, did the rounds as a sex manual, its price of one guinea only being affordable to the better off. Another of his publications was *How to Live for Many Weeks or Months or Years without Eating Anything Whatsoever*.

In a new, but smaller establishment than the Temple of Health, Graham had mud baths installed. These 'earth baths' were often demonstrated by himself, but he also employed young women to demonstrate their benefits.

James Graham was eventually imprisoned for giving obscene public lectures and for libelling Edinburgh magistrates in 1783.

The Edinburgh artist, John Kay, included a drawing of Graham apparently pursuing a Miss Dunbar, in his book of portraits and caricature etchings of Edinburgh people, published posthumously in 1877. Dressed in typical eighteenth-century clothing of the middle classes, Graham sports long boots, white leggings, a long white linen coat, wig and large hat. Who Miss Dunbar was is not known, but apparently Kay sketched the illustration in 1785, and she appears to be running (not too quickly) from his approach, he having a bunch of flowers for her.

Graham changed some of his beliefs in Edinburgh. He now claimed that people should avoid 'excessive sexual indulgence', and that they would benefit from avoiding eating flesh and blood, keeping instead to cold water and fresh milk. All liquor and alcohol was also banned. Fresh air became one of his new wonders, and he applied unsuccessfully to the council to allow him to build a small house on the summit of Arthur's Seat, the great rocky hill that rises in the centre of the city. There he had hoped that he could 'experience the utmost degree of cold that the climate had to offer'.

In Edinburgh Graham found religion, but religion of a different sort. He founded the New Jerusalem Church, but was to remain its only member. He claimed that he was a messenger who had been sent from heaven to advise people on earth how to improve their lives and live in the way that God had intended. After finding religion, Graham signed off all future letters as 'The Servant of the Lord, O. W. L.,' the initials standing for 'Oh, Wonderful Love.'

In 1792 Graham went on a fast for 15 days, during which time he wore clothing that comprised of grass turfs.

Graham must have suffered mentally, and it was not unknown for him to strip off his clothes and give them all to the poor, even if he was in a busy street at the time. On one occasion in 1794 he was arrested for giving away his clothes and walking around naked.

Despite Graham's lifelong obsession with health, both his and others, he took seriously ill in 1794. A blood vessel ruptured whilst he was in a house in Edinburgh's Buccleuch Street. He died suddenly, aged only 49. Despite being scorned as a quack for most of his life, some of his ideas have become more accepted, for magnetism has been used in bracelets and necklaces, mud baths have been used for treating skin complaints, vegetarianism has increased in popularity and hypnotherapy has been used for numerous conditions. Graham, in fact, is often credited with inventing the modern face pack, electrotherapy and even vegetarianism.

# 16

# *The Bogus Minister:*
# *Rev. Thomas Clifford*

On the morning of Saturday 27 August 1910 Chief Constable Lowdon and Detective Inspector Craib made their way to a house at 49 Princes Street, Newton-upon-Ayr, the poorer northern suburb of Ayr. At the house they arrested a man, Thomas Henry Clifford. He was at his mother-in-law's home at the time, and the arrest was made quietly so as not to attract a lot of public attention. Clifford was taken to the police station in the town's Sandgate, where he was held in a cell. The sight of the policemen and their prisoner did not attract much attention in the town as they made their way towards the station, but as soon as word spread around town as to who the prisoner was, the town went into a buzz of gossip that lasted all through the weekend and beyond.

Held in gaol for a few nights, Clifford was taken to the Burgh Police Court on the morning of Monday 29 August where he was formally charged. A massive throng had gathered to witness the event, crowding round the courthouse doorway, but only enough visitors to fill the public gallery were admitted.

The Clerk of Court, Mr T.L. Robb, read out the charge:

Thomas Henry Clifford, 64 John Street, Ayr, the charge against you is that on 12th July 1910 at 239 High Street, Ayr, you did falsely pretend to Alexander Livesey, bookseller, residing there, and Rachel Langlands, residing at 17 Russell Street, Ayr, who were then and there present for the purpose of entering into a marriage, one with the other, and to other persons then and there assembled as witnesses and guests at said marriage, that you were a minister of the Wesleyan Methodist Church, and as such entitled to celebrate marriages according to the forms of the Church, and to act as clergyman or minister in the celebration of marriages, and did celebrate a marriage or act as a clergyman or minister in the celebration of a marriage between the said Alexander Livesey and Rachel Langlands, and did sign the schedule for the registration of said marriage with your signature as officiating minister.

The Burgh Fiscal, L.C. Boyd, requested of the Bailie, Mr Vincent, that the case be remitted to the Sheriff Court because of the nature of the charge, and this was agreed to. As he was being led from the court Clifford nodded at a few of his friends, and managed to shake warmly the hand of one who was close enough. The crowd made their way to the front of the police station to see Clifford depart, but he was not brought out with the rest of the prisoners and led to gaol. Instead he was kept behind for an hour before he was escorted to the prison in a taxi cab by Detective Inspector Craib and Detective Sergeant Paterson. The crowd, who had waited for Clifford to leave, followed the cab to the Sheriff Court in Wellington Square, but again were unable to see him. On Wednesday 31 August a crowd again gathered at the Sheriff Court to see him, but he was not to be brought before the Sheriff-Substitute that day.

The night before his trial, Clifford sat down and wrote a public letter to his congregation which was published on his behalf by the *Ayr Advertiser*:

H.M. Prison
Ayr, 10th October 1910

My Dear People,
I feel it is my duty to write to you at this time, so that I might acquaint you with my future intentions. You know that since my incarceration in prison I have had very little opportunity of doing anything toward the clearing myself of the charges brought against me. This may be my last word to you for some time, but I want to assure you of this truth, that, whatever may be said to the contrary, I am an ordained minister of the Gospel, and, as such, am not guilty of these charges that are libelled against me. To clear myself, and produce proof of these assertions will necessarily mean a journey to London, and the taking up again of my own name. I will never rest now until I have proved to the people of Ayr the truth of my assertions. I call you all to witness to this truth, that I have never held myself out as a Wesleyan minister in the present tense, but have always spoken of myself as having been ordained by that body, and subsequently leaving them for reasons, some of which I have already given you in the past. And yet, this is what I am charged with – Having presented myself as a Wes. Minister I commend you one and all to the Eternal Good, the Great All Father, and I assure you all that you have not heard my voice for the last time. I shall (D.V.) return and take up the work to which God called me, and the people who persecute me to-day shall in the future days be sorry for all that is happening now. May God bless you all, and all who are dear to you. I shall not forget you, but in the dark days of trial I shall be comforted with the thought that someone cares. I thank God for the very little good he has helped me to do amongst you from time to time, and now asking an interest in your prayers and a further portion of your confidence, believe me still your loving Pastor and Friend in the bonds of Christian love.
T.H. Clifford

Clifford was born around 1874, supposedly in Canada, but he moved to England and settled in London whilst still a child. He claimed that he joined the Carl Rosa Opera Company and earned his living as an opera singer until his religious conversion. He then allegedly took various degrees and graduated for the ministry in the Wesleyan Methodist Church. However, Clifford claimed that he and some others severed their connection with that church on account of their conscience, being unable to conform to some of the church's regulations.

As far as the police were concerned, and they had great difficulty in piecing together his early life, Clifford first emerged in 1898, as a soldier. In 1900 he married Florence Palmer and fathered two children with her. However, the marriage was unhappy and Clifford turned to drink. In 1904 Clifford was found guilty of fraud – he lived at the time in a very desirable home in the suburbs of London but he travelled into the city every day and acted out the part of a decrepit beggar, slouching slowly along the streets. He was able to beg considerable sums of money from the unsuspecting public, before returning home each night.

At a later date he lived in Cambridge, where he claimed he was an undergraduate of Trinity College and a nephew of the noted non-conformist clergyman, Dr Clifford. As such he fooled tradesmen and shopkeepers into passing him goods, for which he was sentenced to three terms of two months each.

Florence obtained a separation order from him in 1907, but on a few occasions she had to take him to court for failing to provide financial support. As a result he was held in Brixton gaol from February to April 1909.

On 14 April 1909 Clifford and Ethel Brown travelled on a coach from England to Scotland, and whilst still in the carriage, shortly after crossing the border, he presented her with a ring and placed it on her finger. They arrived in Glasgow and settled at 33, and later 57, Rose Street, Garnethill, then 38 Dalhousie Street, followed by Dunoon, Larbert and Alloa, before moving to Ayr.

They then lived for short spells at Tig Road, Prestwick Road, and Princes Street. When Ethel gave birth to twins on 16 October 1909 at 13 Viewfield Road in Ayr, named Frederick Austin Clifford and Isobel Mildred Clifford, Clifford was aware that his claimed date of marriage would make it obvious to all that his children had been conceived out of wedlock, a position totally unacceptable to a minister, so when registering their births he claimed that he and Ethel were married on 28 February 1909.

Clifford came to Ayr as a representative of the Scottish Protestant Alliance, on behalf of which he delivered a number of lectures against the Roman Catholic Church. The previous representative, Mr MacDonald, had been removed from office as a result of his connection with the police in the sectarian riots organised in Kilwinning and elsewhere. During the summer of 1909 Clifford delivered lectures against the Roman Catholic Church, and decided that the weather agreed so well with his wife's health that they would stay in the town. He therefore broke his connections with the Alliance and commenced his own evangelical mission in the town.

This mission was established around October 1909 and soon there were enough adherents for him to rent the Free Gardeners Hall in the Sandgate. Clifford also organised religious services on the Low Green during the summer of 1910, which many people attended. When advertising these services he used the prefix 'Revd', and added the titles BD and BA after his name.

During the General Election of 1909 Clifford supported the Liberal candidate for the Ayr Burghs, which alienated some of his adherents.

At one of his meetings on the Low Green Clifford's conduct was such that his standing as a minister was questioned, and he was asked by some of his congregation to prove that he was indeed a qualified minister. Clifford asked for some time to obtain a certificate from the Methodist church, and eventually presented one to the committee of his mission on 12 August 1909. Clifford had used the time he was given to print a fake certificate, apparently issued by the Hinde Street Wesleyan Church, Manchester Square, London. This stated that he had been ordained as a minister and various handwritten notes and signatures had been added. He then presented the certificate to the congregation, but they were not educated enough to judge the authenticity of the certificate, and as there was no other Methodist church in Ayr they were unable to compare it with any other certificate.

Clifford also presented the certificate to a local firm of solicitors, and they wrote to the local press, confirming that a copy of the certificate had been presented to them, and that the original could be inspected at Clifford's home.

The question of Clifford's character was raised by the police, and they quietly began taking notes and investigating the matter further.

Clifford appeared before the Hon. Sheriff-Substitute Lockhart at Ayr Sheriff Court on Tuesday 20 September 1910. More charges had been added to those brought before him at the Burgh Court, including that of bigamy. When Clifford appeared before the Sheriff-Substitute he was dressed in his clergyman's clothing. He was only there for declaration, and James Hillhouse, solicitor, acted on his behalf. He applied for bail, which was fixed at £200.

On Tuesday 11 October Clifford appeared at the Sheriff Court, where he was tried under Sheriff-Substitute Shairp. The crowd hoping to attend the trial was tremendous, and many were left outside, unable to gain admission. At around 10 a.m. Sheriff-Substitute Shairp took his seat and proceedings commenced. P.F.P. Fraser MacKenna appeared for the Crown; Clifford was undefended. It was thought that Mr Anderson was going to defend Clifford, but he intimated to the court that he was not going to take any part in the proceedings. The sheriff then addressed Clifford, 'I understand you wish to conduct your own case?'

'Yes, sir, I wish to conduct my own case,' replied Clifford.

Shairp continued, 'You have had a certain charge served upon you which you have read, I presume. Do you wish to have it all read again to you now?'

Clifford thought for a moment then replied in the affirmative. Six charges were then read out to Clifford, namely that he claimed to be a minister of the name of Thomas Henry Clifford, that he conducted wedding ceremonies as though he was a minister, that he produced a false certificate purporting to be from the Methodist Church, that he collected funds for the erection of a church in Ayr, that he married bigamously, and that he registered the births of his twin children as though he and his wife were married.

The sheriff asked Clifford if he pled guilty or not. He responded, 'Before pleading, my Lord, may I ask a question?'

On being given the go-ahead, Clifford asked, 'If I give my real name and address, and the date of my ordination – both these names are libelled as aliases – would this case be withdrawn in its entirety?'

The fiscal informed Clifford that the case would not be withdrawn unless Clifford was able to produce conclusive evidence that the cases did not have a substantial basis. The fiscal stated that Clifford had had since the end of August to prove his case as far as he was concerned, and some time longer as far as the public was concerned, to prove that he was not a bogus minister. Sheriff Shairp then informed him that the Crown wished to continue with the case under his present name.

Clifford then announced that he would plead guilty, with the exception of the fourth and fifth charges, relating to the false representations to the Mission Committee and the charge of bigamy. The sheriff asked the fiscal if this plea was acceptable, and he responded that it was. Clifford then signed the book recording his plea, signing it with the name 'Cecil De Smith'.

The sheriff asked if he admitted the previous convictions, to which Clifford replied that he did, however he wished to point out that the three sentences he received at Cambridge were in fact really only one sentence of six months.

The case continued, whereupon the prosecution put their case forward, that Clifford was guilty of a variety of forms of fraud. Clifford's defence was lengthy. He pointed out that he was in Ayr for five weeks as a layman preacher for the Scottish Protestant Association, during which time he styled himself as 'Mister'. At the end of that time, when he thought of giving up lecturing, he was asked by a number of people to stay in Ayr and found a mission, which he did, again styling himself as Mr Clifford. In his early life he was ordained to the ministry, in fact he was the son of a minister and his brothers were ministers also. He stated that due to a folly on his part, he had to change his name, and that neither Smith nor Clifford was his real name. It was under this third name that he was ordained as a minister. He claimed that it was sometime after the mission had started that he was asked by the members to take the prefix 'Revd'.

Clifford then went on to point out that he took no fee for marrying the couples in Ayr, and neither did he ask for one. The couples had asked him to carry out the ceremony, and before he assented, he researched the law and discovered that in Scotland any man could carry out that part of the religious ceremony so long as the schedules were properly filled out.

As for the certificate proving who he was, he stated that he was not asked to produce this until last June. He claimed that the original certificate was in the safe keeping of a friend, and was not forged, and that the fact was that in his early life he was given such a certificate. He pointed out that the Wesleyan Church did not normally issue the certificate, that he had to apply for it, and should any man, for whatever reason, wish to leave the Wesleyan Church then they could apply for the certificate to prove his ordination. During his speeches he had stated that he had at one time been in the ministry, and when this was questioned he wrote to the secretary of the Wesleyan Methodist Conference, asking for the certificate that he duly received. He then took the certificate to his solicitor, who suggested publishing it. It had not been his idea. Clifford pointed out that there were in fact two certificates, one was a printed copy and the other had the name of ministers written on it.

Clifford then went on to explain about the money he collected during his services and for his work as a minister. He originally had a salary of 30 shillings a week, but on starting the mission he gave this up on the promise of no fixed salary. He was just to take what came in. He informed the court that there were many present in the courtroom who could vouch for the fact that he often took home figures as low as 2s 6d, 8s or 9s a week. He admitted that he commanded large audiences at his meetings on the Low Green, usually attracted by his good singing voice, and he did agree with the accusation that he earned seven guineas on one day alone. However, this figure was duly presented to the treasurer who wrote it up in his books. By the agreement of the mission, what he earned at his meetings on Mondays, Wednesdays and Fridays went in his own pocket, what he earned on other days belonged to the church. He made sure that he pointed out to the audience where the money was going to at each meeting, and that the sum raised was always counted in the presence of the audience.

Clifford told the court that he had given up a salary of 30 shillings a week when the mission moved into the Free Gardeners Hall, after which he only received a small amount of cash, and he often had to receive gifts of food. He explained that he did in fact earn any money that he was given, pointing out that since taking up the position as pastor in the mission he had made over 1,000 visits to the homes of the poor and had given help to the homeless and hungry.

As far as the charge of bigamy was concerned, he stated that he was indeed husband to Florence Palmer, but within three years of his marriage he was led astray by some men who influenced him into gambling. To keep up with his debts he got involved with moneylenders, and things went from bad to worse. He admitted to obtaining money by posing as a beggar, but this was only to prevent the moneylenders from selling his house. However, he did end up in prison, during which time his wife deserted him and in 1908 informed him that she was starting divorce proceedings.

Clifford claimed that his marriage to Ethel Amy Brown was Scriptural, and that he did not agree with many of the forms of marriage used by various churches. He stated that not all marriages had to conform to that laid down in civil law, and he was satisfied that he was lawfully married to Ethel.

Clifford concluded by stating that any sentence he should receive he would serve cheerfully, but would like to point out that he did not deserve it. He admitted to deserving the punishments he had received in his past, but these had been paid for by terms in prison. He claimed that he was now being persecuted, and that he did not deserve the present proceedings against him. He had tried to do his best as a minister in Ayr, and asked that his Lordship would bear in mind that he had a wife and child to support (one of the twins having died in infancy).

In Sheriff Shairp's summing up he described the case as one of the worst that had ever come before him and he sentenced Clifford to 18 months' hard labour. After he read the sentence Clifford responded by almost inaudibly saying 'Thank you'. It was noted that in court Clifford had an air of nonchalance throughout, and did not seem to appreciate how severe the charges laid before him were. Prior to the case being brought up he talked freely with those he met and read his morning paper. As he was led away to gaol he smiled at those he knew in the gallery.

After his release from prison, Thomas Clifford spent most of his time earning a living as a racing tipster. He often appeared at Ayr Racecourse and other racecourses throughout Scotland, selling racing tips to the public. Clifford's second wife died in 1921, leaving him with three young children to bring up. His wife had been a devout Christian, and it is reckoned that she was instrumental in keeping him on the straight and narrow for some time. He was often to be heard on Glasgow Green giving out tips, and could earn around £45 to £50 on a Sunday. However a by-law was passed in Glasgow that prevented him from carrying this on. He was also a regular orator at Hyde Park in London and afterwards sold his tips outside the park gates. But around June 1927 he moved to Newcastle. Clifford would often listen to the various preachers who held meetings in public locations. Among those he heard were Spurgeon, Parker, Jowett, Talmage, Meyer and General W. Booth. On one occasion Hugh Price Hughes came down from the platform in St James's Hall and placed his hand on Clifford's shoulder, making a personal appeal to him.

When Clifford arrived in Newcastle he quickly established himself as a tipster and could draw in £40 in two or three hours on a Sunday morning. During the week he went to local market towns where he carried out the same sort of work. On one occasion his tipping was disrupted by a group of Gospel preachers. On another occasion he was returning home on the bus when he was tapped on the shoulder by Rev. Ledger Pawson. They talked for the remainder of the journey and Pawson appealed to Clifford's better nature to consider the error of his ways. Clifford began to attend mission services on Sunday evenings from then on, both in church halls and in the open air.

Around September 1928 Clifford returned home one night and, as he opened the door of his house, he saw his youngest daughter, who was by this time eight years of age, kneeling on her bed with his eldest daughter sitting by her side. The youngest daughter was saying her bedtime prayers and she prayed for her sisters, and ended her thoughts with 'And, O God, make daddy a good man.' This so touched Clifford that he was born again once more. He gave up tipping and found a legitimate occupation. It was also noted that 'all desire for drink has left him'. Clifford resumed preaching and spoke at the Wesley Hall and Newcastle Palladium along with Rev. Stanley Parker of the Newcastle Mission.

# 17

## *An Absolute Tissue of Forgeries: James MacPherson*

The great English lexicographer, Dr Samuel Johnson (1709–84), and his trusty sidekick, James Boswell (1740–95) of Auchinleck, took themselves on a tour of the Scottish Highlands and Islands in the autumn of 1773. Johnson was keen to see this wild part of Scotland, and Boswell was keen to show off Scotland, as well as to take Johnson to his home at Auchinleck. As they journeyed the topic of conversation at one point turned to the hugely successful literary epic of the time, the *Poems of Ossian*. These had appeared in Edinburgh in 1760 as *Fragments of Ancient Poetry collected in the Highlands of Scotland* and had been translated by James MacPherson, who had found various pieces of ancient Gaelic poetry, extolling the early heroes of Gaelic mythology, and telling tales of battle and combat won by the great hero, Fingal. This poetry was supposedly written by a third-century bard named Ossian.

Dr Johnson was adamant that the poems 'never existed in any other form than that which we have seen', referring to the English translations produced by MacPherson. Boswell, like many others who admitted that the whole poem could not be a translation from a single work, thought it possible that MacPherson had added intervening verses to tie up the fragments that perhaps did exist. Johnson also described *Fingal* as 'a mere unconnected rhapsody, a tiresome repetition of the same images. In vain shall we look for the *lucidus ordo* [clearness of order], where there is neither end nor object, design or moral, *nec certa recurrit imago* [no definite image recurs].'

One of the great lexicographer's quotations makes reference to the poems of MacPherson. He is reported as having said that the poems had little merit – 'Sir, a man might write such stuff forever, if he would *abandon* his mind to it.'

MacPherson was angered at Johnson's comments, and wrote almost immediately to him, threatening all sorts of legal action. Johnson, however, was unperturbed and his reply to MacPherson appeared in a variety of contemporary newspapers. It read:

Mr James MacPherson, – I received your foolish and impudent letter. Any violence offered me I shall do my best to repel; and what I cannot do for myself, the law shall do for me. I hope I shall never be deterred from detecting what I think a cheat, by the menaces of a ruffian.

What would you have me retract? I thought your book an imposture; I think it an imposture still. For this opinion I have given my reasons to the publick, which I here dare you to refute. Your rage I defy. Your abilities, since your Homer, are not so formidable; and what I hear of your morals, inclines me to pay regard not to what you shall say, but to what you shall prove. You may print this if you will.

Sam. Johnson.

MacPherson did not reply to Johnson's letter.

The controversy surrounding the authenticity of the Ossianic poems was one that rocked eighteenth-century Britain. The Scots, who had been politically joined to England since the Act of Union of 1707, found much of their Highland culture suppressed following the Jacobite Rising of 1745 and the defeat of Bonnie

Prince Charlie at the Battle of Culloden in 1746. They grabbed at the 'discovery' of part of their ancient culture – that Scotland appeared to have an older literary tradition than England was a great boost to national pride.

James MacPherson was born at the clachan of Ruthven in Inverness-shire in 1736, the village of which has since disappeared. He came from a well-to-do farming family, his father being Andrew MacPherson, a relation of the Cluny MacPhersons, chiefs of the clan. Following some education at home he was sent off to Inverness Grammar School with the intention of studying for the church. He showed considerable talent there, resulting in his parents sending him to King's College in Aberdeen in 1752, followed by Edinburgh University. In 1756 he taught at the charity school at Ruthven. At the same time he had his first book published, a poem in six cantos entitled *Highlander*. Based on a mixture of Greek and Gothic mythology, it was rather poor in quality, and did not find success. MacPherson later acknowledged just how bad it was, and tried to suppress it. He also wrote a number of other verses, some of which were published in *The Scots Magazine*.

Whilst working as a tutor in the south of Scotland MacPherson met Rev. John Home (1722–1808), author of *Douglas*, a verse tragedy, and he told him of the fragments of Ossianic poetry he had come across. *The Death of Oscar* was produced by MacPherson in 1759 and Home was so impressed by it that he circulated it widely amongst his literary friends. MacPherson was advised by Home to gather and translate as many fragments as he could. At first MacPherson wasn't enthusiastic, claiming that no translation of his could do justice to the originals, and that as they were of a different style to modern poetry the public may not like them. However, he was told by Hugh Blair, Professor of Literature at the University of Edinburgh, that if he could gather enough fragments of poetry together then he would arrange for them to be published in a small book.

Having completed his studies, and perhaps qualifying as a minister, MacPherson pulled all of his bits of poetry together to produce a work entitled, *Fragments of Ancient Poetry, collected in the Highlands of Scotland, and translated from the Gaelic or Erse Language.* Containing 15 short poems, with an anonymous preface that was in fact written by Blair, in which he describes the importance of the pieces, the book was printed in Edinburgh in June 1760, and instantly drew the attention of the great and learned of Scotland and beyond. The verses were received with great enthusiasm and sales of the book were phenomenal.

One of the first to query the honesty of the poems was Thomas Gray, who wrote to Horace Walpole in April 1760:

> I am so charmed with the two specimens of Erse poetry, that I cannot help giving you the trouble to enquire a little farther about them, and should wish to see a few lines of the original, that I may form some slight idea of the language, the measures, and the rhythm.

As the editor claimed that there were many other fragments of Gaelic poetry awaiting translation, it was determined that there should be a public subscription to raise enough funds to allow MacPherson time to collect and translate these pieces. The principal patrons in this fundraiser were Dr Hugh Blair (1718–1800), Dr William Robertson (1721–93), Dr Alexander Carlyle (1722–1805) and David Hume (1711–76). At the time James Boswell also subscribed to the fund, having found the original verses had 'wild peculiarity'. The effort made by these individuals led an air of credulity to the project, and MacPherson lost no time in travelling around the Highlands, searching for more pieces of the great Ossianic legend. He spent most of his travels in the north-western parts of Inverness-shire, the Island of Skye and some adjacent islands.

On 17 October 1760 MacPherson wrote to Rev. James

MacLagan, minister of Amulree, then Blair Atholl, 'I have met with a number of old manuscripts in my travels, the poetical part of them I have endeavoured to secure.' He wrote to the minister again on 16 January 1761, 'I have been lucky enough to lay my hands on a pretty complete poem, and truly epic, concerning Fingal.'

If the whole epic poem by Ossian could be collected and put together, then Scotland would have established herself as one of the earliest of modern cultures, with an unrivalled classical literature. It would also prove to be a swipe at the English, for there was no equivalent ancient epic poem in the English tradition.

Having toured the Highlands and Islands MacPherson made his way to Edinburgh, where he set about turning what he had found into a book. He lived at that time in Blackfriars Wynd, immediately below the home of Blair. It is reckoned that MacPherson did much of the translation from Gaelic, and that Blair assisted in polishing the final English copy. This appeared from the press of William Strathan in London in 1762 as *Fingal, an ancient Epic Poem in six books; together with several other Poems, composed by Ossian, the son of Fingal: translated from the Gaelic.* Yet again the public thought these verses to be brilliant, and sales of the title were massive once more. MacPherson was feted as a great hero, one who had saved the poems from being lost, and one whose translations allowed them to be enjoyed by a wider audience. The story of the poems spread beyond Britain, and soon much of Europe was enthralled by the books, with translations being made into most European languages, including German, French, Italian, Swedish, Danish, Polish and Russian.

*Fingal* was a major contributor to the Romantic Movement which spread throughout Europe. Various writers and composers, such as Johann Wolfgang von Goethe (1749–1832) and Richard Wagner (1813–83) produced a new form of literature and music. Byron, Wordsworth and Tolkien all owe some debt to

MacPherson. *Fingal* was so highly regarded by Napoleon Bonaparte that he is said to have carried a small volume of the poems with him everywhere he went, even into battle. Indeed, they are said to have influenced his decision to re-establish the Scots College in Paris, which had been destroyed during the French Revolution, and his summer house, the Malmaison, had paintings from the poems within it.

The whole Ossianic craze swept through Scotland, in particular the Highlands, where any tenuous link with the tradition was seized upon and elaborated. A classic example is Ossian's Hall, or the Hermitage, near Little Dunkeld in Perthshire. Now owned by the National Trust for Scotland, this folly was erected high on a rock overlooking the tumbling Braan, which roars in its gorge 40 feet below. At one time the window in the summer house was fitted with a sliding panel, on which was painted a vision of Ossian, which could be suddenly swept to one side, revealing the breathtaking view down the gorge.

The names Ossian and Fingal became fairly common with the popularity of the poems, much in the same way as today's footballers and pop stars have many children named after them. Oscar Wilde (1854–1900), the famous Irish writer and poet, was in fact baptised Oscar Fingal Wilde, Oscar being the son of Ossian in the verses.

Another volume of MacPherson's poems appeared in 1763, entitled *Temora, in eight books, with other Poems, by Ossian*. This was not as successful as the previous two volumes, but was still well received. However, it was around this time that questions began to be raised regarding the authenticity of the poems. Other scholars began searching for original Gaelic verses and could find none – they couldn't find any evidence of MacPherson's original poems either. According to Johnson:

> The editor, or author, never could shew the original; nor can it be
> shewn by any other; to revenge reasonable incredulity, by refusing

evidence, is a degree of insolence, with which the world is not yet acquainted; and stubborn audacity is the last refuge of guilt. It would be easy to shew it if he had it; but whence could it be had?

Johnson reckoned that the Scots who claimed to have heard fragments of the poem in their youth were misled, and were not necessarily lying. He admitted that the same fraud could have taken place in England, claiming that he could write an epic poem on the story of Robin Hood and that 'half England, to whom the names and places he should mention in it are familiar, would believe and declare they had heard it from their earliest years'.

Following the questioning of MacPherson's honesty, his manner began to change considerably. Even his friend David Hume found him to be disagreeable. Hume wrote to Dr Blair, asking him 'not to mind so strange and heteroclite a mortal than whom I have scarce ever known a man more perverse and unamiable'. MacPherson had become insolent and conceited, a change that seems to have been quite sudden.

The Highland Society of Scotland commissioned an enquiry into the possibility of the existence of some ancient Gaelic poems. The enquiry was undertaken by Henry MacKenzie, noted as the author of *The Man of Feeling*, and was published in 1806. In it MacKenzie noted that there were indeed ancient Gaelic verses, and that these had been collected by the Dean of Lismore between 1512 and 1529. He translated more than 2,500 lines of poetry, published as *The Book of the Dean of Lismore*. This book had been used by MacPherson. MacKenzie also commented that where MacPherson had made up the intervening lines, these were in no way as good as the original verses.

The Highland Society came upon many Highlanders who claimed that they knew of the poems before MacPherson had translated them. One man, Rev. Andrew Gillie of Kincardine parish in Ross-shire, stated, 'Before Mr MacPherson could know his right hand from his left, I have heard fragments of them repeated, and many of those fragments I recognised in Mr MacPherson's translations.'

In 1764 MacPherson moved to Pensacola in America, where he worked as secretary to Captain Johnstone, governor of that territory. After helping to set up the civil government there, he fell out with Johnstone and decided to return to Britain in 1766. He had gained a pension of £200 per annum.

MacPherson settled in London, and again turned to literary pursuits. He produced *An Introduction to the History of Great Britain and Ireland* in 1771, a volume that drew much criticism from all over, claiming that the book was poor and flawed in many places. MacPherson responded that he wrote the book merely for private amusement, something that may well be true, for he was still earning considerable amounts from the sale of his Ossianic poems.

In 1773 MacPherson produced a translation of *The Iliad* by the legendary Greek epic poet, Homer. As soon as it came out of the printer's workshop critics lambasted it. Learned men laughed at it, and the *Critical Review* pulled it to shreds. Despite some positive comment from Sir John Elliot, the book failed. It took MacPherson some time to rebuild his reputation with other publications. Other works were more successful, such as *A Short History of the Opposition during the Last Session of Parliament*, which appeared in 1779, and *The History and Management of the East India Company*, published in the same year.

MacPherson was elected as Member of Parliament for Camelford in Cornwall in 1780, and was re-elected in 1784 and 1790. He was not much of an MP, for he did not speak one word in the House of Commons.

With his fortune made from the sales of his poems, MacPherson was able to purchase the estate of Balavil, sometimes spelled Belleville, which lies to the north-east of Kingussie in Inverness-shire. There he employed Robert and James Adam to design a country house, erected in 1790–6 on a wooded hillock. This was built on the site of the ancient castle of Raitts. Despite his interest in the ancient heritage of Scotland and the vogue for castellated mansions at the time, MacPherson adopted the classical style for his house. It is reckoned that the cost of the house was around £4,000.

The house and estate were much ornamented. Within the house there was a hall of shells, and he commissioned Sir Joshua Reynolds to paint his portrait. A landscape of the house and grounds were painted by Rev. John Thomson of Duddingston. In the library were a number of fine leather-bound books, including three bound in gilded morocco leather, gifted by the Prince of Wales. The grounds, which included the lands of Banchar, Clunes, Phones, Invernahavon and Etteridge, were well planted with trees, and around the immediate policies he planted hardwood trees and an avenue of elms.

At Balavil MacPherson was much admired. He did much to improve life for the poorer tenants on his estate, and was the first to pay agricultural labourers one shilling per day. He spent some time campaigning to have the forfeited estate of Cluny MacPherson returned to him. This had been attainted following the Jacobite Rising in 1745 and Cluny MacPherson had been deprived of it since. With 'Ossian' MacPherson's help, the estate was restored to Duncan MacPherson of Cluny (13th Chief) in 1784. The government had actually offered the estates to 'Ossian' MacPherson, but he preferred that they were restored to their rightful owner. At Knappach, near Ruthven, MacPherson erected a new house for his mother, though she complained that he should not spend so much money building houses on land that he did not own.

MacPherson's health began to decline and he decided to retire to Scotland where he hoped the clear air would bring about a return to good health. He made his way back to Balavil. He died there on 17 February 1796, at the age of 60.

MacPherson made sure that he would be remembered when he was gone. He had amassed a considerable fortune, and £1,000 of this was left to John MacKenzie of Fig-tree Court the Temple, London with which he was to print another edition of *Ossian* in the original. MacPherson also left £300 for a memorial to himself, to be erected on some prominent point near to Balavil. This was constructed on a low knoll at Lynchat, and later MacPhersons were buried around it. It is a classical memorial, a slate obelisk topped with an urn finial. On the north face is a crest of white marble, a portrait of MacPherson and a carving of a mourning lady.

MacPherson also left money so that his corpse could be taken to London and buried in Westminster Abbey. A special coffin was made to transport the body. The inner container was made from Scots pine grown in Glen Feshie, the surrounding container was made from lead, and the outer coffin was manufactured from mahogany. The coffin was transported south and was laid to rest in Poets' Corner.

Although MacPherson was never married, he left behind four natural children, who were amply provided for by means of his will. The eldest, James, succeeded to the estate. Another son, Charles, had died in India.

The controversy regarding the poems of Ossian was one that occupied the literati of the period. Both sides of the argument were adamant that they were right in their opinions, and the evidence produced resulted in the upper hand passing from one side to the other for some time. The debate even resulted in essays being written in support of each opposing side, and in 1781 'An Inquiry into the Authenticity of the Poems of Ossian', appeared, written by W. Shaw. Of the contemporary publications, it is reckoned that six came out in favour of the authenticity of the poem, whereas five found against this.

Those who supported MacPherson analysed the verses and were convinced that the style of writing contained many examples of antique forms of writing. They also claimed that there were many people across the Highlands who could recite some of the original Gaelic verses on which the translation was based. Dr Blair published a 'Dissertation' on MacPherson's poems, ranking them with the poems of Homer and Virgil and defending their authenticity. Others who supported MacPherson included philosophers David Hume and James Beattie (1735–1803). Hume noted that Walter MacFarlane, the greatest antiquarian in Scotland at the time, insisted strongly on the historical truth of the verses. Some supporters reckoned that although the bulk of the poems were genuine, MacPherson had taken some poetic licence and had in fact interpolated the original fragments with numerous verses composed by himself. Even supporters of MacPherson used the author's poorer quality in his other works as proof that these poems were better than that of which he was capable!

Sir Walter Scott wrote that he conferred with a number of Gaels regarding the Ossianic poems, and 'you would far sooner have got them to disavow the Scripture than to abandon a line of the contested tales.' This willingness to question the Bible rather than to deny the existence of Ossian-type early Gaelic verses, proved that devout Christians believed in the existence of the original poems. However, Scott also wrote that he was 'compelled to admit that incalculably the greater part of the English Ossian must be ascribed to MacPherson himself, and that his whole introductions, notes, etc., etc., are an absolute tissue of forgeries.'

Sir John Sinclair of Ulbster (1754–1835), famed as the compiler of the *Statistical Account of Scotland*, in which every parish in the country was analysed and its current condition reported in great detail, also produced a 'Dissertation on the Authenticity of the Poems of Ossian', published in 1806. In this he supplied the original Gaelic verses on which Ossian was based, that had been gathered from across the Highlands. It has been claimed that these verses, compiled by a man so determined to record accurately the state of the country in 20 volumes, must be proof of the existence of the Ossian poems, for he had nothing to gain, and a great reputation as a scholar to lose, by supporting a fraudulent poet.

MacPherson acknowledged at one time that he did in fact add some of his own verses to the poems. He was challenged by Dr MacIntyre of Glenorchy and accused of being the author of the bulk of the work. MacPherson replied, 'You are much mistaken. I had occasion to do *less* of that than you suppose.'

Those who claimed that the poems were false had one great ace up their sleeves. MacPherson was regularly challenged to produce evidence of the existence of the Gaelic verses on which his translations were based. He consistently refused to reveal these, and did so for 30 years after the publication of his verses.

Horace Walpole began to tire of the poems, complaining that he was fed up reading 'how many ways a warrior is like the moon, or the sun, or a rock, or a lion, or the ocean . . . I cannot believe it genuine.' In February 1781 he wrote to William Mason that he had now decided that the Ossian poems were 'dull forgeries'.

Once MacPherson had died, scholars were able to study his collections. It became apparent that he had discovered a number of original verses in the Highlands, but that the bulk of the poems of Ossian were in fact written by himself, and that he had taken fragments of poetry and created an epic around them.

The existence of Fingal, Ossian and others in the poems, has sometimes been claimed by referring to place names and objects which bear their names. Fingal's Cave on the tiny island of Staffa is a classic example. A large cavern surrounded by columnar basalt rock formations, the cave became a major tourist attraction. It even inspired Felix Mendelssohn to write his *Hebrides Overture*, following a visit there in 1829. However, the cave was only 'discovered' in 1772 when Sir Joseph Banks came this way on his return from Iceland on advice from a Mr Leach. Banks named the cave after Fingal, assuming that the great hero had some connection with it, but in fact it had been historically referred to as An Uamh Binn, or the melodious cave.

Many other places that claim to have associations with Fingal are in fact prehistoric sites. There is Fingal's Fort, or Dun Fionn, which is located in the parish of Kiltarlity, near to Beauly. A vitrified hill fort, it was partially excavated in Victorian times. Another Fingal's Fort can be found at Corriegills on Arran. Fingal's Griddle is an ancient stone circle that is located at Ormsaigmore, in the parish of Ardnamurchan, Argyll. Another stone circle can be found on the island of Arran, known as Fingal's Cauldron Seat. Fingal's Oak was an ancient tree that grew near to Barcaldine House, in Ardchattan parish, Argyll. Fingal's Seat, or Ait Suidhe Thuin, is a mountain at the head of Loch Portree in Skye, on which Fingal supposedly sat, surveying his heroes around him. Fingal's Stair is a stair-like rock structure on the slopes of Beneaddan, to the south of Loch Sunart. Fingal's Limpet Hammers can be seen on the island of Colonsay – again they are ancient standing stones.

Ossian's Stone, or Clach na Ossian, is supposedly the spot where Ossian was buried. The stone, which is located in Glen Almond in Perthshire, was moved in 1728 when General Wade's Military Road was being laid through the pass. Under the boulder, which stands eight feet tall, was discovered a stone kist, in which were bones and ashes. According to Thomas Newte, who came this way in 1791 and recorded in his *Prospects and Observations on a Tour in England and Scotland*:

I have learned that when Ossian's Stone was removed, and the coffin containing his supposed remains discovered, the people of the country for several miles around, to the number of three or four score of men, venerating the memory of the bard, rose with one consent, and carried away the bones, with bagpipes playing and other funereal rites, and deposited them with much solemnity within a circle of large stones, on the lofty summit of a rock, sequestered, and of difficult access, where they might never more be disturbed by mortal feet or hands, in the wild recesses of western Glenalmond.

Ossian's Cave is a narrow slit on the rock face of Aonach Dubh, overlooking Glen Coe.

A few places are named in honour of Fingal's dog, Bran. The Dog Stone at Dunollie, near Oban, is claimed to have been where the dog was tied up. Another stone with this legend, the Clach a' Bhacain, can be seen in Glen Lyon, Perthshire. On Arran there is a large prehistoric stone structure which legend claims was Fingal's daughter's grave. Other locations are named in honour of Diarmid, who was admired by Fingal's wife and who was killed by Fingal.

Although the Great Highland Hoax is really nothing of the sort, MacPherson's poems no longer have anything like the popularity they had at one time. Nevertheless, the poems of Ossian as translated and embellished by James MacPherson still remain in print, and even some of those translated into foreign languages are still available in book form.

# 18

## The Perfect Hosts:
## Monty and Martha Spencer

The thought of a major film being shot at the ancient castle of Airlie in Angus was met with considerable excitement on the estate and in the locality. Cameramen were filming the epic picture *Rob Roy*, starring Liam Neeson, in Perthshire, with a number of scenes set at Drummond Castle, with its extensive and unique formal gardens. It was indicated that Neeson would be coming to Airlie, in order to film some scenes for the movie, and word spread quickly around Airlie parish and beyond, to Kirriemuir in Angus. The tenants of Airlie Castle informed the housekeeper, Barbara Jackson, of what was happening, and what the filmmakers expected.

Accordingly a number of removal vans turned up at the castle one day, and most of the antique furniture was removed from the castle and loaded into the vans. It was stated by the tenants that the makers of the film wished to use the interior of the castle, and that they would furnish it with items that tied in with the period of Rob Roy MacGregor, the famous Scots freebooter who lived in the eighteenth century. Aberdeen removal firm, Clark & Rose, emptied much of the castle, packing up many priceless antiques in boxes and taking them away. Two large articulated lorries were eventually filled, and the drivers were instructed to take the items to a new house the tenants had taken on in London.

The tenants of Airlie Castle at the time were Monty and Martha Spencer, a couple who appeared to have plenty of money, and a significant amount of time on their hands. They became involved in the social circle of the district and, as well as inviting guests to their home, were often asked to attend functions in the county.

Some of the furniture was packed by the removal firm and taken north to a storage depot in Aberdeen. Some of the better-quality antique furniture, up to half of the contents, was kept aside and sent south to London. At one point Monty Spencer telephoned the removal company to inform them that his new flat was not ready yet, and could the furniture be redirected to a storage depot in Wembley. The manager of Clark & Rose tried to persuade them to use a facility that they themselves had in London, and which would have formed some kind of guarantee that the Spencers would pay the £16,000 removal bill, or else their belongings would not be released. However, Spencer was adamant that it should be taken to the other storage company. The manager of the removal firm contacted the Airlie estate to check that moving such a bulk of furniture was in order, only for them to confirm that the Spencers were decent folk, and that everything should be alright.

The filming party arrived at Airlie, but the shoot did not involve major scenes within the castle that would have required it to be empty, indeed, the shoot did not involve the inside of the castle at all, only some still publicity shots of Liam Neeson and Natasha Richardson were taken for use within *Vanity Fair* magazine.

The Spencers did not return, and soon the housekeeper began to wonder where they had gone. She was unable to contact them, and they did not contact her. After six weeks had passed, and payment of the rent had stopped, the estate administrators made their way to the castle and entered with spare keys. They found the interior stripped bare. The police were contacted, and the story of the Spencers' sudden departure with the bulk of the contents of the castle began to unfold.

Airlie Castle is a mixture of buildings of various periods, perhaps the oldest surviving part being the entrance gateway and adjoining ten-foot thick wall, which were probably erected in 1432 when Sir Walter Ogilvy of Lintrathen received a licence from King James I to rebuild the 'Tower of Eroly'. The gateway has a sandstone tower with conical turret, which dates from the sixteenth or seventeenth century. The castle, known in history as the 'Bonnie Hoose o' Airlie', occupies a magnificent location on a promontory high above the confluence of the River Isla with the Melgam Water, six miles west of Kirriemuir. It is reached down a half-mile-long driveway from the gatehouse at the public road. The Earl of Argyll burnt the castle to the ground in 1641, during the Bishops' Wars. It then lay in ruins for over 100 years, the Ogilvy family moving to nearby Cortachy Castle, which they still own. In 1746, after the Jacobite Rebellion, King George II confiscated the estate and Lord Airlie lived in exile. He was eventually allowed to return from Versailles and undertook the task of rebuilding the castle. He brought with him some French masons and attached a Georgian country house to the castle's remains in 1792–3.

Part of the extensive Airlie estate, Airlie Castle was occupied by the Dowager Countess of Airlie, widow of the 7th Earl, up until her death in 1984. The Earl then signed over the castle to his son and heir, David John Ogilvy, who was born in 1958. David Ogilvy, who has the courtesy title of Lord Ogilvy, worked as a managing director of an art dealership in London, and also has a career in music. He has released two solo albums, *Like It Is* and *Mockingbird,* and wrote a pop song, performed by another artist, which earned him a considerable amount.

Being based in London, David Ogilvy had little need of an

ancient castle perched on a rock in Scotland. He contacted the Edinburgh office of Knight Frank & Rutley in 1987 and asked them if they could find a tenant for the castle. With what seems to have been great luck, within a short time an American couple visited the offices of the estate agents in the capital's Fountainbridge and asked if there were any large country houses or castles available for let in the Highlands. The couple appeared well dressed, and they spoke with rather refined American accents.

The agent, Colin Strang Steele, was well-aware of Airlie Castle and presented it to Monty and Martha Spencer as a possibility. They were very interested, and negotiations for the lease went on apace. The Spencers produced references from banks across the world, including some in the United States, France, and even Coutts in London, celebrated as bankers to the royal family. Confirmation of their ability to take on the lease was also produced in letters from solicitors. It was later claimed, when things had gone wrong, that Knight Frank & Rutley thought that the estate's solicitor had carried out the relevant checks on the Spencers, whereas the solicitor claimed that it was the estate agent's job to do this.

In any case, for a number of years there was little to indicate that the Spencers were not what they appeared. The estate was delighted to find that the rent, which was in the region of £18,000 per annum, was paid on time with cheques drawn on Coutts bank. The Spencers also seemed to develop a circle of friends from the upper classes, all of whom regarded them as genuine. Among these was Sir James Cayzer, 5th Baronet, who lived eight miles to the south at Kinpurnie Castle, near the village of Newtyle in Angus. Lady Kinloch of Kinloch (d. 1997), an elderly woman who lived nearby, invited the Spencers to lunch. Another acquaintance was Baroness Strange, owner of Megginch Castle in Perthshire, who was a noted author. The Spencers also met and claimed as a friend Sir Robert Lindsay, 29th Earl of Crawford, who had met them in Cambridge. The Earl of

Mansfield, owner of Scone Palace, also dined with them, as did the Earl of Perth from Stobhall Castle and the Countess of Strathmore from Glamis Castle.

Monty Spencer was a rather jolly looking chap. He was not particularly tall, being described as a chubby teddy bear. He sported a small goatee beard and his age, which was never really confirmed, was thought to be in the region of 60. He said that he came from Washington DC and had made his money in real estate, buying properties that could be rejuvenated or subdivided into flats, and selling them on at a profit. Recalling some of his conversations later, one of the Perthshire locals said that Monty claimed to have purchased his first flat whilst still a student, and that he worked up to buying whole blocks of apartments. He claimed on other occasions that he was in fact a lawyer who specialised in international law.

Martha Spencer, his wife, or at least it was always assumed that it was his wife, appeared to be in her thirties. She usually had a large smile, and her reddish hair was worn short at the sides, but often bouffant on top. Martha claimed to have a sister who lived in Cambridge, hence her visits to the old university city.

The Spencers did not sleep together, hinting that the pair, between whom there was a considerable age difference, may not have been married, and were merely a pair of con-artists. When they lived at Airlie, Monty Spencer used one of the large double bedrooms in the castle, whereas his wife spent the night in a single bedroom further down the corridor. They were distinguished in the locality by the powder-blue Rolls Royce in which they drove through the Perthshire countryside.

The Spencers became involved in the social circle of the county. They were invited to lavish dinner parties, and they returned the compliments by inviting the neighbouring gentry to meals at Airlie. Parties in the castle were always a delight, and the Perthshire gentry were more than happy to accept invitations to meals or functions held in the ancient castle.

The food supplied at Airlie was always of the highest quality, for Martha Spencer delighted in being an accomplished chef. At Airlie she held cookery demonstrations, along with Mary Contini, of the famous Edinburgh restaurant and delicatessen, Valvona & Crolla. She even took part in BBC Television's programme *Masterchef*, winning BBC Scotland's Masterchef of the Year in 1992, (she went on to the British final before being beaten). Probably born in New England in 1953, Martha was educated in Massachusetts.

Monty Spencer claimed that he came from an old family, one that had left Britain many years ago and settled in various parts of Europe before emigrating to the United States. Sir James Cayzer was even persuaded to take Monty on trips with him to St Moritz in Switzerland and to Sweden, where he was supposedly tracking down the graves of his ancestors.

The Spencers became proud of their castle home, and one day whilst in the woods on a walk they met Lord Airlie's brother, Sir Angus Ogilvy, and his wife, also enjoying the woodland walks. Sir Angus had married Princess Alexandra, daughter of the Duke of Kent and cousin of Queen Elizabeth II. The Spencers invited them in to Airlie, to let them see around the house and grounds. Princess Alexandra later recalled that the Spencers had been a charming and warm couple, and were only too keen to please.

In June 1994 Martha Spencer took ill, and had to be taken to a nursing home in Dundee for recuperation. Sir James Cayzer went to visit her, and was surprised to be told by Monty that his wife was suffering from cancer, and that she did not have long to live. He told Sir James that there was a chance of saving her, if only he could get her to America where they were performing an operation that could help. The hospital, however, required a deposit towards the considerable costs of the treatment, and was asking for £50,000 to be paid in advance. Monty claimed that he was unable to raise the funds at the time, as all of his cash was tied up in various funds. He asked if Sir James could lend him the money so that he could book in Martha as soon as possible.

Sir James told Monty that he would see what he could do. By luck he spoke to his nephew, Nigel Cayzer, who told him to think seriously about lending such a large sum of money. Sir James explained the story of Martha's illness, but the nephew was soon very sceptical, for his wife and Martha shared the same gynaecologist, and he denied that Martha had any serious ailments.

The Cayzers agreed that they would offer a guarantee instead. Accordingly, on 20 August 1994, Sir James telephoned Monty at a flat he had taken on in Grosvenor House Apartments in London, to let him know. The Spencers had rented an apartment in the upmarket, gated residence from 11 August until 27 August. Located on the edge of Hyde Park, the apartments are within easy reach of the haute couture shops of Bond Street, and offer personal staff and 24-hour room service. The bill was paid on their departure by credit card, one that apparently had funds at the time.

The last confirmed sighting of the Spencers in Angus took place on 6 August 1994, when they attended the opening of the gardens at Kinpurnie Castle, home of Sir James Cayzer. The castle, which was built by Sir James' great-grandfather Sir Charles Cayzer between 1905–7, stands in magnificent grounds on the northern edge of the Sidlaw Hills.

Also left behind were two dogs that belonged to Martha Spencer. The terriers were named Mabell and Bridget, names that Martha had taken from the late 6th and 7th countesses. Martha had asked the housekeeper to look after the dogs until she returned, but she never did.

Whilst in London the Spencers visited Selfridges, Liberty, and many other expensive shops, making purchases of numerous quality items. The list of unpaid credit accounts with these shops was tremendous. Many of the items were regular domestic purchases, such as furniture and appliances, but the Spencers also bought a pair of his and hers Rolex Oyster watches. They also bought a pair of shotguns, valued at £42,000. When the owner of the shop sent faxes to Airlie Castle requesting that the outstanding bill be paid, his faxes were being re-directed to Switzerland, where Monty Spencer was receiving them and immediately consigning them to the bin.

Soon rumourmongers began guessing why the Spencers had done a bunk. One of the stories doing the rounds was that the Spencers were international drug dealers, and that their regular visits abroad were simply to stock up on drugs for the British market. Another popular theory was that the Spencers were upmarket burglars. With their circle of friends in surrounding castles, they knew exactly how to gain entry, and when their owners were likely to be out. At the time the Spencers were at Airlie there were a number of high-profile thefts from Scottish country houses. Floors Castle near Kelso in the Borders was broken into and some fine paintings removed. Similarly, a forced entry was made into Scone Palace near Perth, and again a number of valuable antiques were stolen. Some people claimed that the Spencers were involved in such raids, and that they were stealing items to order for unscrupulous foreign collectors.

It was also claimed that the Spencers had treated Airlie Castle as their very own property, and during the time that they leased it, they sold a number of valuable portraits and antiques to fund their lifestyle. The bulk of the quality antiques that had been sent to Wembley for storage were gradually removed from the depot, taken away in a small non-descript white van. The valuation of what was taken was reckoned to be around £250,000.

The investigation soon discovered that the Spencers had left behind a massive trail of debt. In fact, the amount they owed totalled £1.5 million. Monty had purchased a diamond ring from an Edinburgh jeweller, telling the managing director, Julia Ogilvy, that he did not use credit cards, and instead obtained it on credit with the shop. Julia, who is married to James Ogilvy, the son of

Sir Angus Ogilvy, stated that Spencer's credit had previously been good, but as soon as he purchased the ring, suddenly it was not. Some claimed that the ring that he 'purchased' from the jeweller's was worth as much as £60,000.

Not all of those who had been in contact with the Spencers were convinced that this had been an elaborate long con. They had been at Airlie for ten years, which was quite a build-up to the point when they disappeared with the castle contents. Ken Jackson, the housekeeper's husband, reckoned that something serious had suddenly happened to them. Perhaps they had lost millions in a financial deal that had gone wrong, forcing them into exile. It was claimed that their credit rating was checked one week and it was okay, whereas the next it was definitely not.

An arrest warrant for the Spencers was issued by Forfar Sheriff Court in 1994. Tayside Police contacted Europol and Interpol, and after some time Martha Spencer was tracked down to Miami in the United States, where she had set up a new life under a different name. Other accounts claim that she was living in a holiday resort in New England. At the time the police decided not to pursue her extradition as it was hoped that she would be able to direct them to the whereabouts of her husband.

Martha Spencer disappeared once more, and it was not until 2002 that she was discovered, living on a remote island in the Pacific Ocean. A television company, making a documentary on the Spencer case, found her working on the island as a volunteer teacher. Despite intensive searches around the globe, Monty Spencer was never found. The documentary was shown as part of the BBC Scotland series *Ex-S* in 2002.

The arrest warrants that were issued for Monty and Martha Spencer were dropped in May 2006. Originally issued at Forfar Sheriff Court, the Crown Office withdrew the warrants, but would not explain why it had done so. The dropping of the warrant angered Phil Gallie MSP, who had been active for almost ten years in trying to push the police in the case. One of his constituents was a friend of the couple, but he claimed that 'the Spencers could now escape.' Gallie raised the matter at the Scottish Parliament, concerned that a considerable amount of money had been spent on trying to track down the Spencers. Gallie said, 'If this is the way the Crown Office sees as a good method of reducing crime figures, by simply clearing the books, then it's not good for those of us who still believe in justice.'

# 19

# *The Bogus Lord:*
# *Lord Glencairn and Gordon-Gordon*

A very well turned-out gentleman made his way into a respected goldsmith and jeweller's shop in the city of Edinburgh. It was sometime in 1868, and he stood around five feet ten inches in height. He had curling brown hair, bluish eyes and mutton-chop whiskers. He wore a silken hat, patent leather shoes and gloves. The jewellers, Marshall & Sons, sold a variety of expensive jewels, from diamond rings and gold watches to pearl necklaces and gold lockets. Making his way to the counter, the gentleman greeted the jeweller as he removed his hat and gloves.

He requested to see some rings, and the jeweller brought out a tray of fine diamond rings and placed them on the counter. As the customer browsed among the trinkets and gold bands, he made conversation with the jeweller.

He told him that he was around 25, that he was the rightful Earl of Glencairn, and that he was due to inherit on 25 March 1870, which would bring him a massive fortune. He had letters from a solicitor based in Lincoln's Inn in London, that appeared to confirm that he would indeed inherit the Glencairn title and estates valued at £100,000 at that time.

The Earldom of Glencairn was created in 1488 for Alexander

Cunynghame, Lord Kilmaurs. The title passed through 14 earls, but on the death of John Cunninghame, 15th Earl of Glencairn, in 1796 the title became extinct. Or at least, it is thought that the title became extinct, it is more likely dormant. A number of lesser families claim to be descended from younger sons of the early earls, and the title may yet be revived if one of these can prove to the Lord Lyon King of Arms, Scotland's premier lord in matters heraldic, that they have a rightful claim to the title. At present it is thought that the Cuninghames of Corsehill have the most likely claim to the peerage.

The shopper selected a few rather fine items of jewellery, and persuaded the jeweller to open an account in his name. The account was duly opened, and Lord Glencairn returned to the jeweller a number of times over the following year.

One day the jeweller realised that Lord Glencairn had not been in for a while, and that he still had a considerable account to settle. He decided to look in his large accounts book just to see how much was owed, and was taken aback at the figure jotted down. Glencairn had built up a massive debt and had not been to the shop for many months to pay anything towards the items purchased.

When another titled man appeared in Marshall & Sons' premises, the jeweller asked him if he knew Lord Glencairn. He replied that he didn't, but the name rang a bell. He would make inquiries and return. When he did come back to the jeweller, it was as the bearer of bad news. Investigations around Edinburgh resulted in the conclusion that there was currently no such title as Lord Glencairn, and no one could think of who the man was. The jeweller had been swindled out of hundreds of pounds worth of stock.

Lord Glencairn had also taken on the lease of some important grouse and deer-stalking estates in Angus. There he became acquainted with the minister of Glenisla Parish Church, Rev. J.W. Simpson, who was later to supply some evidence in the bogus lord's trial in New York:

My dear Sirs:

For reasons which you can easily understand, I do feel a reluctance to give evidence against our former friend 'Lord Glencairn,' but I also feel that it would be very unjust to you to withhold any information I can give you. I proceed to do so as shortly as I can. He first appeared here in June or July '68. So far as I can recollect, he then passed under the name of Hamilton and had a small shooting in this neighbourhood. No one knew anything of him, and there was much surmising as to who he was, but as he paid his bills punctually, lived quietly and had the manners of a gentleman, no one could find anything against his character or conduct. He left about the end of the season, having taken a larger shooting for the following two seasons. He returned next August and then appeared under the title of 'Lord Glencairn'. During the previous season he threw out hints to those with whom he came in contact, that he was something grander than he seemed to be. To myself he said that he had a place in Lanarkshire and another in Ayrshire, but that he had not good health at either of them. He also hinted that he had property in Northampton, in England. His manner was not to tell any one directly who or what he was, but to make statements which led you to infer that he was a man of title and had property in various places in Scotland, England and Ireland. When he returned in July, '69, as Lord Glencairn, there were grave doubts as to his character. His own account of his title was plausible – that his grandfather had left money in chancery – an immense sum, to him, on condition that he should take up the title of Glencairn when he reached the age of 27; that he was now of age and must take it up; that his agents in London had nearly completed the process, and he would in a few months be served heir to his grandfather and to the earldom of Glencairn. He did not speak to me of his Scotch estates, but often hinted of his property in Northampton and at the immense sums in chancery.

There were things about him I could not well understand, but as he continued to behave in a gentlemanly way and had friends from England with him who were men of standing and respectability, and especially as he was certified to be a man of rank and wealth by his lawyers, a well-known firm in Lincoln's Inn, I was willing to think the best of him, and at least to wait until he discovered himself before I judged him. And he did discover himself. His estates in Scotland and England turned out to be pure falsehoods, his claim to the Earldom, whatever it was, ended in nothing.

No process in pursuit of it had been entered even in any of the law courts of England or Scotland, and though he left very little unpaid debt in this quarter, yet I know that he swindled various parties elsewhere out of large sums.

I could enter more into detail, but it is unnecessary. I may shortly add that as in all material points his pretensions to rank and property turned out to be utterly false and untrue. I can consider him nothing else than an impostor, and yet who or what he is I know no more than the first day I saw him.

With much regard, I am,

My Dear Sir,

Very truly yours,

J. W. Simpson.


In the city of Dundee Lord Glencairn opened a bank account, persuading Robert Yeaman, the bank manager, that he had an income of between £40,000 and 50,000 each year. Yeaman appears to have been one of very few who was not taken in by the bogus lord, for he refused to grant him an overdraft.

The debts run up by Glencairn were considerable. He owed his solicitor £5,000, Marshall & Sons were owed £300, and there were many other businesses in Edinburgh, Angus and London that had supplied goods on credit and were now counting the cost of their stupidity. Many of the jewellery items that Glencairn had 'purchased' had been given to various friends, and on his disappearance they decided to return them to Marshall's shop, thus reducing his loss to £116.

Meanwhile, Lord Glencairn had emigrated to the United States, disappearing before the date in March 1870 when he claimed his inheritance would allow him to pay off his debts. He had changed his name, adopting the strange title 'Lord Gordon-Gordon'. By now he had acquired an even more aristocratic ancestry, claiming to be connected to the Earl of Aberdeen, the youngest member of the House of Lords, and a descendant of George Gordon, Lord Byron, the great nineteenth-century romantic and poet. He claimed to be a cousin of the late Marquis of Hastings (died 1868, when the title, conveniently for Glencairn, became extinct), a relation of the Duke of Hamilton, and a friend of the Prince of Wales, later King Edward VII.

Gordon-Gordon then moved on, arriving in Minneapolis, in the state of Minnesota, in the summer of 1871. Where he had been for the intervening 15 months is not known. He made his way to the city bank, where he opened an account under his aristocratic name. The bankers were taken aback, but were absolutely delighted, when he deposited $20,000 worth of British notes. He took up lodgings in the main hotel in the city, registering as G. Gordon. However, within a few days a letter arrived at the hotel, addressed to Lord Gordon-Gordon. The hotel clerk spotted that he was titled, and soon most of the 20,000 residents knew that he was in town. He was regarded as something of a lion, many residents entertained him, and he was invited to many private and public functions, where he became a celebrated public speaker.

In Minneapolis Lord Gordon-Gordon announced that he proposed creating a new town or city in the state, located on the banks of the Pelican River. He claimed that he had an option on 25,000 acres of plain which would be divided into farms. To work these it was his intention to bring over 300 people from his estate back in Scotland. In the centre of the area he would create a new town, with businesses and industry. At the centre of town he proposed erecting a large bank to deal with the funds that would be generated by the businesses that blossomed here, and on another side of the town square would be a massive hotel, able to supply accommodation to visiting businessmen.

Within the area where Gordon-Gordon proposed his new city was a small village that was gradually growing, named Pelican Rapids, in Otter Tail County. Living there was an early pioneer of the state, W.G. Tuttle, who had arrived from Rochester in New York State. He had staked a claim to 80 acres along the side of the river and had erected a store, where he was trading in all sorts of goods. Across the Pelican River he had created a dam, with the intention of using the water to power a sawmill. Tuttle's timber cabin was distinguished by one amazing item of furniture for the mid-west at the time – a baby grand piano. This had been hauled across country to keep his wife happy, for she was an accomplished player. The cabin became one of the major centres of public entertainment in Pelican Rapids, with dances, sing-alongs, and concerts all relying on her playing.

Gordon-Gordon persuaded Tuttle that he should come on board with his grand plans. Tuttle was taken in, and even agreed that the dam that he had constructed was too inferior for the proposals, and set about building a larger one. The lord told Tuttle that he had sufficient funds to build a massive city, and that he proposed renaming the village Loomis, in honour of Colonel John Loomis, who was the land commissioner of the Northern Pacific Railroad Company.

The Northern Pacific Railroad Company was seriously in need of a major investment of capital, and Loomis reckoned that a partnership with Gordon-Gordon could help the business. Loomis and Gordon-Gordon set out on an expedition through the state to decide on the best location for the new city, and to scout out where railroads could be created in order to link the city with the rest of the United States network. The land was to be staked out, and claims to it lodged. The whole expedition, which was most elaborate and expensive, was funded by the railroad company. It had 'a caravan of forty horses, twelve men to pitch tents, a French cook and a number of coloured waiters wearing white linen aprons and white silk gloves', according to a contemporary report. Another account states that Gordon-Gordon travelled in royal state, with two wall tents for his own use. He had a man who acted as a valet and secretary, and in the expedition party was one wagon filled with hunting and fishing equipment. However, once the directors of the company discovered what Loomis and Gordon-Gordon were doing they called a halt to the plans. Loomis was dismissed from his job, and it was calculated that the railroad company lost $30,000 by working with Gordon-Gordon.

Once Tuttle had built a new dam and sawmill, Gordon-Gordon told him to cut down acres of forest, in order to supply timber for building homes for the hundreds of Scots he intended bringing over. Tuttle wasn't sure about cutting down the trees at first, for he knew that they had been granted by Congress to the St Paul Pacific Railroad. Some of the woods would be used for a right-of-way, others would be cut down and sold to pay labourers who were employed in laying the new tracks.

Gordon-Gordon told Tuttle not to worry, for he had an option on the land, and was going to take it up soon, giving him all rights to the timber. Somewhat convinced, Tuttle borrowed money from a fellow businessman and friend, George Robison of Wisconsin, and commenced cutting down trees and logging. Throughout the winter of 1872 he produced millions of cubic feet of sawn timber.

Gordon-Gordon by this time had moved on. The railroad company came to claim back their timber from Tuttle. They asked him to pay for what he had cut down and converted. Already heavily in debt to Robison, he was unable to clear his bill. To prevent losing his livelihood he passed the mill to Robison, whom he regarded as a friend, using the funds to pay off some of his creditors. However, within a short time Robison sold the mill to R.L. Frazee who evicted Tuttle. Other creditors came and took possession of Tuttle's cabin, leaving his furniture in the open. The baby grand piano was sold and the money raised was just enough to allow the Tuttle family to travel to New York. Tuttle was totally broken by his debts, and died in a New York asylum in 1882.

After returning to Minneapolis, Lord Gordon-Gordon headed east to New York in February 1872. He had with him a letter of introduction to Horace Greeley, a notable politician, who established and was the editor of the *New York Tribune*. It was he who uttered the famous line, 'Go West, young man,' and he was delighted to meet the aristocrat who appeared to have taken his advice and had great proposals for opening up the West.

At the time of Gordon-Gordon's visit, there was major rivalry between the United States railroad companies. Jay Gould (1836–92) was one of the major players in the industry, making millions of dollars dealing in stocks. He is also noted as being a founder of Western Union, but there was a murky side to his business dealings as well, and his attempts to corner the gold market resulted in the original Black Friday, when millions of dollars were wiped off the stock market. Gould was in the process of trying to maintain sufficient stock in order to keep control of the Erie Railroad Company, with the intention of using it to develop new routes across the North American continent. He had acquired control of the firm in 1868 by a manipulation of shares, something that the other directors were totally against. Lord Gordon-Gordon claimed that he owned 60,000 shares in the Erie Railroad Company, vital shares that would make a massive difference to Jay Gould's presidency of the company. Gould wanted to entice Gordon-Gordon onto his side and in a panic gave him 600 shares of Erie, around 1,900 shares of other businesses associated with Erie, 4,722 of the Oil Creek and

Allegheny Valley Railroad, 21,000 dollar bonds of the Nyack and Northern Railroad, and $160,000 in cash. Gordon-Gordon took the package, but claimed that it was $40,000 short. He reported the error to Gould, who returned with the sum in cash. Whilst in Gordon-Gordon's hotel room he asked for a receipt, to which Lord Gordon-Gordon responded in an indignant manner, claiming that his word of honour should be good enough. He handed the pile of bonds and dollar bills back to Gould.

Gould walked away with the cash as far as the hotel room door. There he stopped, turned around and returned to Gordon-Gordon, handing him the bundle and announcing that he reckoned the money was in safe hands.

Gould's purchase of support in the company was soon seen to be futile. Gordon-Gordon began selling some of the stock in the markets, resulting in Jay Gould losing control of the railroad company. Gould discovered that a stock-broker in Philadelphia was selling his Oil Creek and Allegheny stock at a much-reduced price – indeed, by 1872 Gould's shareholding dropped to less than that required to keep control of the company, and it was soon being run by others.

Gould and a party of men, including the New York chief of police and a police justice, went to Gordon-Gordon's hotel and camped outside the room. Gordon-Gordon was persuaded by an intermediary to open the door, whereupon Gould demanded that Gordon-Gordon repay the funds and stock that he had been given. Horace Greeley of the *New York Tribune* persuaded Gordon-Gordon that he should return the securities, for failing to do so would result in immediate arrest. To avoid such an indignity, Gordon-Gordon handed over what remained of Gould's stock package. However, when Gould counted up what he had been given back he discovered that he had been short-changed by £150,000. In an attempt to recover the money, Gould took out a summons against Gordon-Gordon, and the case went to court on

17 May 1872. Gordon-Gordon took out a counter-case against Gould, but this was not followed through.

Prior to the trial Gordon-Gordon was asked to supply bonds, or bail, to ensure that he would attend court. On the first day of the trial in the Supreme Court of New York he stood in the witness box and answered the questions with dignity. He informed the sheriff that his lawyer was based in England, and supplied the court with his name and address. He gave details of who his family were, and of well-connected friends and relatives in aristocratic circles in Scotland, France and Switzerland. At the end of the first day the court was adjourned, to resume the following day. Jay Gould's counsel, David Dudley Field, sent telegrams to all the names and addresses in Scotland that had been supplied by Gordon-Gordon, but was to discover that none of them existed. Gordon-Gordon, however, absconded, catching the overnight train from the United States into Montreal, Canada. His bondsmen, who had assured the court of his appearance, lost $37,000 in bail money.

Lord Gordon-Gordon took the railroad from Montreal west through Ontario to Winnipeg in Manitoba. In October 1872, when he arrived, the city did not exist, and a small community known as Fort Garry stood there. This was a trading post run by the Hudson Bay Company. Gordon-Gordon spent the next few months living there, spending most of his time hunting in the forests. He took up lodgings with Mrs Abigail Corbett at Headingley. He still claimed to be Lord Gordon-Gordon, a mistake that was to lead to his capture.

During the summer of 1873 some men from Minneapolis were in Winnipeg on business and spotted Gordon-Gordon in the street. They sent word of the aristocrat's presence back across the American border to Minneapolis. In July 1873 a group of men from the state of Minnesota decided to carry out an expedition to try to capture him. The mayor of the city, George A. Brackett, had been persuaded by Gould's lawyers to arrange the kidnapping, and he appointed Captain Mike Hoy, a marshal in Minneapolis, and Owen Keegan as the leaders. They made their way to the headwaters of the Mississippi River before crossing the 47th Parallel and entering Canada. On 2 July 1873 they were able to find Gordon-Gordon and kidnap him.

The abduction took place at the home of Hon. James MacKay, where Gordon-Gordon was visiting. MacKay was away from home, and his farmhands had drunk too much and were unable to prevent the kidnapping. Gordon-Gordon had his hands and feet bound, and the party set off through Fort Garry and the Pembina trail, heading for the United States.

However, a rescue party in Canada was formed and they set off in pursuit. Just 100 yards short of the boundary they caught up with the abductors. The Americans were arrested, for they had no right to be in Canada, and abducting a man, even a fugitive from justice, from Canada was against the law. Hoy and Keegan were held in Canadian gaols for many months for their part in the attempted abduction. One of the party, Loren Fletcher, sent a cable back to the USA, stating, 'I'm in a hell of a fix. Come at once.'

A number of Americans responded to his request; Mayor Bracket headed to Winnipeg by train to try to sort things out. A message was also sent by the American consul in Winnipeg, stating, 'Two detectives from Minnesota attempted to arrest a person "Lord Gordon" in New York proceedings by Jay Gould. Did not consult me. I have not seen their papers. Detectives arrested near Pembina for kidnapping and just arrived here.'

The tussle between the Canadian and American governments went on for a number of months. Some folk recommended attacking Canada – 'swift, silent and terrible.' Others claimed that the Canadian authorities' refusal of bail to the Americans was particularly hostile. The difficulty was discussed by courts in the state of Minnesota, in the province of Manitoba in Canada, and at the American and Canadian parliaments. There were even claims that the Canadians had arrested the Americans within the United States, and thus they had been acting illegally. However, once a precise astronomical survey was carried out on the spot, it was confirmed as being in Canadian territory. Another claim was that the American warrant was valid as a common-law right and that it could cross international boundaries. The argument was even discussed in Great Britain, where Gordon-Gordon had come from. The dispute escalated and was beginning to affect national relations between America and Canada.

At length the President of the United States, Ulysses S. Grant, and the Prime Minister of Canada, Sir John A. Macdonald, had a discussion regarding the situation, and peace was restored to the negotiations. A court sitting was called for 16 September 1873, at which the Minnesotans were found guilty and sentenced to 24 hours in jail. The men from Minneapolis, Hoy and Keegan, were released from gaol, and when they returned to their own city they were treated as heroes, over 2,000 people coming out to see them walk alongside two marching bands and a troop of the Irish Rifles.

In the meantime, Lord Gordon-Gordon stayed in Fort Garry, feeling confident that the treaties between the United States and Canada did not cover the extradition of anyone wanted for fraud. Defending Gordon-Gordon was Henry Joseph Clarke (1833–89), a lawyer and politician in Manitoba, which province he helped establish in 1870. His public defence of Gordon-Gordon was to become a complete embarrassment for him later, when the lord was denounced as a fraud. He was to lose his position in the Manitoba ministry in July 1874 and resigned as Attorney General. Later he was making his way to California when he was attacked by a number of investors who had lost heavily in one of Gordon-Gordon's schemes. He was left with some severe injuries.

The story of Lord Gordon-Gordon had again reached the

British Isles, and the Edinburgh jewellers, Marshall & Sons, began to wonder if this could be the same person who had swindled them some years previously as Lord Glencairn. They sent their clerk, Thomas Smith, to Canada, to identify Gordon-Gordon. With a positive recognition, a warrant for his arrest was issued.

On discovering that he was now a wanted man on yet another front, Lord Gordon-Gordon decided to take his own life. At the time he was boarding once again with Mrs Abigail Corbett, and on 1 August 1874 the police arrived at the house. Lord Gordon-Gordon was present, and seemed to accept his arrest. He packed a bag of belongings and then excused himself on the pretext of going to his room to collect a warmer coat for the long journey. When in the bedroom he took a pistol and held it to his head. The shot killed him instantly.

Just who was Lord Gordon-Gordon? There are conflicting theories, and so far none has been proven. One story claims that he was the son of a rather well-to-do couple, or at least who appeared to be respectable, but who, in fact, had a secret life running a smuggling business on the island of Jersey.

Another story claims that he was an illegitimate son of the manse. The tale claims that he was not the minister's child, but was born from a union between the minister's son and the maid who worked in the manse. When it was discovered that the maid was pregnant she would have been dismissed by the minister, but when the minister found out who the father was he decided to send them both off to a new home in a different county, where the future 'lord' was brought up.

A third story claims that Lord Gordon-Gordon was really someone named John Hamilton. He had worked as a butler in a large country house where he was able to learn how the gentry lived and worked. A fourth story claims he was really Hubert Campbell Smith, a lieutenant in a Scottish regiment that had served in India for some time.

The story of Lord Gordon-Gordon was written into a full-length opera in two acts by Victor Davies in 1968. A tale of romance and humour, entitled *Let us Pay Tribute to Lord Gordon-Gordon,* the opera has many witty songs and attractive melodies, but ends, like the story of Lord Gordon-Gordon himself, in tragedy.

# Index

212

Hall, Hector 68
Hamilton, Francis Buchanan
109–10, 113
Hamilton, Lady Emma 158
Hastie, James 69
*Herald, The* 123, 125
Heriot 2–3
Hermitage, The 179
Highland Destitution Relief Board
43–8
Highland Society of Scotland 180
Hill, George 36–7, 39–40
Hippisley, Gustavus Butler 69–70
Home, Rev. John 176
*Honduras Packet* 67–8
Hood, James 32–4, 37–9, 41
Hoy, Mike 208–9
Huddersfield 99–102
Hume, Andrew 99–103
Hume, David 177, 180, 184
Hume, Grace 97–104
Hume, John 101
Hume, Kate 97–105
Hunter, Patrick 76–7, 84–5
Huntly 127, 129

Innes, Andrew 71, 87
Inverardrine 59
*Inverness Courier* 43
Irvine 73–8, 84–5

Jersey 210
Johnson, Dr Samuel 174–5, 179–80

Katterfela, Mr 159
Kay, John 160
Keegan, Owen 208–9
Kennedy, John Stewart 140–1
*Kennersley Castle* 67, 69
Killin 106–7
Kilmarnock 32–42, 90
*Kilmarnock Standard* 38, 42
Kilmaurs 78

Kinloch, Lady 191
Kinnell House, Killin 107–8, 112
Kinnell Lodge, Canada 109, 111,
113–4
Kirkcudbright 85
Kirkgunzeon 86
Krashny, Anton 4–5

Laird o' Drumblair 127
*Laird, The* 22
Lannion 117
Larghill 86–7
Lauder, Alexander 45–9
Lee, Brandon 119–25
Leith 67
Loch Ness 23–31
*Loch Ness* 29
Loch Ness Monster 23–31
London 9–11, 21, 65, 90–2, 107,
131, 150–4, 165, 172, 181, 183,
189, 194, 201
*London Magazine, The* 139
Loomis, Colonel John 203–4
Los Angeles 14
Lustig, 'Count' Victor 15
Lyon, Emma 158

Macaulay, Catherine 156
MacGregor, Gregor *Boidheach*
58–60
MacGregor, Josefa 60, 64, 70
MacGregor, Sir Gregor 58–70
MacHardy, William M.F. 127–8
McIlwraith, 'Sir' Alan 51–7
MacKay, Hon. James 209
MacKenzie, Henry 180
MacKenzie, James 138–40
MacKenzie, Peter 45–7
MacKinnon, Brian 118–26
MacLeod, Norman 118, 120–1, 123
MacLeod, Rev. Dr Norman 44
Macnab 109, 114
MacNab, Alexander 112